THE PRESCRIPTS OF ATHENIAN DECREES

MNEMOSYNE

BIBLIOTHECA CLASSICA BATAVA

SUPPLEMENTUM QUADRAGESIMUM NONUM

ALAN S. HENRY

THE PRESCRIPTS OF ATHENIAN DECREES

LUGDUNI BATAVORUM E. J. BRILL MCMLXXVII

THE PRESCRIPTS OF ATHENIAN DECREES

BY

ALAN S. HENRY

LUGDUNI BATAVORUM E. J. BRILL MCMLXXVII

ISBN 90 04 05429 4

PRINTED IN THE NETHERLANDS

To Elizabeth

CONTENTS

LIST OF TABLES

PREFACE

In this study I attempt to trace the development of the prescript of the decrees passed by the Athenian boule and demos. No such comprehensive analysis has been attempted since the Americans began their epoch-making excavations in the Agora, although the years since 1929 have seen the available material substantially and significantly increased. It would now seem an appropriate moment to set down within the compass of a single volume a detailed examination of the history of the prescript.

The idea of this study was conceived of many years ago and owes much to the encouragement, in various ways and at various times, of two scholars in particular, Professor K. J. Dover and Mr. A. G. Woodhead. During the actual period of writing both have made themselves available for consultation and discussion. Mr. Woodhead also performed the invaluable service—and at a time of great personal grief—of reading and criticising an earlier draft. In similar generous fashion he made available to me sections from his forthcoming study of the decrees and ephebic texts from the Agora (*The Athenian Agora*, vol. xvi).

Acknowledgement must also be made of the helpfulness and efficiency of the staff of the Epigraphical Museum in Athens. On two all too brief visits my labours were considerably lightened by the expert attention which was so generously afforded me by the directrix, Dr. D. Peppas-Delmousou, and her colleagues.

Details of earlier enquiries of this kind will be found mainly confined to the Bibliography. Since these works were in the main published even before the advent of the *Editio Minor*, my debt to them is of a general kind, and I have thought it best to present my study *de novo*, with little or no cross-reference to these predecessors in the field. A major debt, however, is to the epigraphists who, over the last 45 years, have faithfully and accurately published the new finds from the Agora. Their names will appear again and again in the following pages. Among them Benjamin Dean Meritt, the doyen of Attic epigraphy, deserves special mention and thanks, in particular for making available an advance copy of his forthcoming revision of the archon list. I am likewise most grateful to John S. Traill, who very generously supplied me with information on his revision of the text of *Hesperia* xliii 1974, 246-259.

I wish also to record a debt of gratitude to three institutions: the Myer Foundation, which in 1967 furnished me with the wherewithal to visit Athens and Cambridge; Monash University, which granted me a sabbatical year in which to complete these researches and later provided a substantial subsidy towards the costs of publication; and the University of St. Andrews, *alma mater carissima*, which generously afforded me facilities for study throughout the calendar year 1975.

Finally, my thanks are due to the editors of *Mnemosyne* for their willingness to publish this work; to the staff of E. J. Brill for their magnificent handling of a most difficult manuscript; and to my colleague, Mr. G. G. Betts, for his great kindness in volunteering to help with the proofs.

September, 1977 ALAN S. HENRY

PROCEDURAL NOTES

(1) *Terminology*: Since there is no universally accepted terminology for the various parts of a decree, I explain here, for the sake of clarity, the terms I employ for the purposes of this study.

A decree may be considered as consisting of three parts:

a) The superscript: At the top of many stones may be found a heading, often in larger letters and inscribed with wider spacing, providing a title to the document. Such headings basically fulfil two functions: (i) they may give an indication of the contents of the accompanying text (e.g. by naming the individual or state affected by the decree, or by specifying the nature of the business transacted); (ii) they may furnish the names of officials (secretary and/or archon). A third type of heading is the single word θεοί, usually inscribed in normal or smaller letters, spaced out across the width of the stele. The precise significance of 'Gods' is not completely evident, but it clearly implies a hoped-for divine sanction for the business in hand. I give the tag 'superscript' to all or any of these items.

b) The prescript: This is properly everything inscribed between the end of the superscript and the beginning of the actual decree. It conveys the details of the meeting at which the decree was enacted, and is normally concluded with ὁ δεῖνα εἶπεν, the mover of the motion.[1] The items of the prescript are an integral part of the final minute of the decree as drafted by the secretary.

c) The decree proper: The actual terms of the resolution and the considerations which prompted its enactment are the third and principal section. In this study we will not be directly concerned with the decree proper or with any amendments to it.

(2) *Dating*: The value of epigraphical evidence is greatly diminished if one cannot assign a reasonably secure date to it. Fortunately, we now have a more or less complete archon list to the end of the Hellenistic period, and many archons are known even in the

[1] I have followed the traditional view which associates the mover with the other items of the prescript. It should be noted, however, that J. Bingen, *Le Monde Grec* (*Hommages à Claire Préaux*) 1975, 470-479, makes a good case for considering the orator as part of the motion which follows.

succeeding centuries (see Appendix I). It has been my policy to accept without query archon dates thus established. Likewise, where dates of a more general nature have been assigned by editors (on grounds of script, historical reference and the like), I have, except in a very few instances, accepted these uncritically.

(3) *Citation of texts*: Epigraphical texts are constantly being re-edited, supplemented or merely reproduced in other publications. In particular, the texts of the *Corpus* are more likely than not to have cross-references in *Hesperia* and the *Supplementum Epigraphicum Graecum*. All this is liable to cause confusion, especially amongst the uninitiated. In order, therefore, to retain the *Corpus* reference and at the same time to indicate the latest (and, one hopes, best) text, I have adopted the practice of citing the *I.G.* number followed by the new reference in brackets. The reader should go to that latter reference to find full details of the discussion contained therein. (Note that, in general, *SEG* is cited in preference to *Hesperia*).

In citing a text from the *Corpus* the letters *I.G.* will normally be omitted. Thus $i^2 1$ = *I.G.* vol. i (*editio minor*), no. 1.

In citing a text from *Hesperia* the year of the volume will not be mentioned, only the page reference and the serial number (if any) of the inscription. However, when referring to an *article* in *Hesperia*, the normal conventions will be observed and the reference will be given by year as well.

In citing a text from Tod (*Greek Historical Inscriptions*) the orthography of the stone will be employed.

If more than one decree is contained on the same stone, Roman capital numerals will be used to mark the distinction.

All dates are B.C. unless otherwise indicated.

ABBREVIATIONS

In addition to the standard abbreviations I have also employed the following (see Bibliography for full details). Except where otherwise indicated, the numeral following an abbreviation will be the serial number of the inscription.

AA	Dinsmoor, *The Archons of Athens in the Hellenistic Age.*
Ag.xv	Meritt and Traill, *The Athenian Agora, xv: Inscriptions: The Athenian Councillors.*
Ag.xvi	Woodhead, *The Athenian Agora, xvi: Inscriptions: Decrees and Ephebic Texts* (forthcoming).
BM	Bradeen and McGregor, *Studies in Fifth-Century Attic Epigraphy.* (References usually by chapter or page.)
D	*A.T.L.*, II.
H	*Hesperia.* (References in the form *H.* xxx 8, 1 = *Hesperia* vol. xxx, page 8, number 1.)
ML	Meiggs and Lewis, *A Selection of Greek Historical Inscriptions to the End of the Fifth Century B.C.*
PM	Pritchett and Meritt, *The Chronology of Hellenistic Athens.*
Pečírka	Pečírka, *The Formula for the Grant of Enktesis in Attic Inscriptions.*
Prytaneis	Dow, *Prytaneis, Hesperia* Suppl. i 1937.
S	*Supplementum Epigraphicum Graecum.* (References in the form *S.* x 18 = *SEG* vol. x, number 18.)
Sokolowski [1962]	Sokolowski, *Lois sacrées des cités grecques* (*Supplément*), 1962.
Sokolowski [1969]	Sokolowski, *Lois sacrées des cités grecques*, 1969.
TAY	Meritt, *The Athenian Year.*
Tod	Tod, *Greek Historical Inscriptions.*

CHAPTER ONE

TO THE BEGINNING OF THE FOURTH CENTURY[1]

The scope of the material available for a study of the prescripts is very wide indeed—from the last years of the sixth century before Christ to the beginning of the third century of our era, a span of some 700 years. Not unexpectedly, however, the distribution is very uneven, with the bulk of the material falling in the period 400 to 100 B.C. For the approximately 200 years covered in this chapter it is important to be aware of the extremely small amount of extant documentation, some 60 to 70 prescripts well enough preserved to permit analysis. Only one of these falls in the sixth century, approximately ten in the first half of the fifth century: as that century progresses, however, there is a steady increase in the number of texts available, but, even so, one is still dealing in terms of tens, not hundreds. There is therefore no question of producing tables of statistics: rather we shall attempt to observe and describe the early steps taken by the Athenians along the road to documentary standardisation and sophistication.

Any study of Athenian decrees must take as its starting point the decree relating to Athenian settlers on Salamis, $i^2 1$ (ML 14), dated probably in the late sixth century.[2] The text of the decree proper depends directly on, and is introduced by, the simple formula of enactment ἔδοχσεν τõι δέμοι. No other details are given: no reference to the secretary or proposer, and no indication of date, unless we follow Luria[3] in restoring vs. 12 to yield a postscript reference to the eponymous archon:

[ἐπ]ὶ τε̃ς B[o]λε[χλέος ἀρχε̃ς].

Meiggs and Lewis prefer [ἐπ]ὶ τε̃ς β[ο]λε̃[ς ....c. 11....], in order to include mention of the boule, and Meritt[4] has filled the lacuna

[1] The chapter divisions of this study have been determined partly by considerations of convenience, partly by reference to the first (or last) examples of particular phenomena.

[2] It is not my purpose to enter into controversy over dates. In the main I shall accept the date offered by the editor of the text I cite.

[3] *Kadmos* iii 1964, 88-107.

[4] *H.* x 1941, 305-6.

with ταῦτ' ἐγνόσθε in an attempt to show that the decree originated as a probouleuma. All this is speculation, however, and no firm procedural inference should be drawn from so isolated an example of this early date. What matters for the study in hand is that the embryo 'prescript'—if it is worthy of so dignified a title—is confined to the formula of legal validation, 'the People resolved.'

i²3 and 4, the Hecatompedon inscriptions, of 485/4, are equally laconic in their lack of detail. Strictly speaking, they lie outwith the scope of our examination inasmuch as they show no prescript at all. However, insofar as they provide one of the few examples of decrees of the early fifth century and contain a postscript [5] which appears to serve the same function as the enactment formula of the Salamis inscription, their evidence can hardly be ignored. In the last two lines (vv. 26-7) of i²4 we find:

ταῦτ' ἔδοχσεν ⁝ τõι δέ[μοι ἐπ]ὶ Φι[λοκράτος ἄρχοντ] stoichedon 38
ος ⁝ τὰ ἐν τοῖν λίθοι[ν τούτ]οιν.

and the same provision has been restored in i²3 at vv. 16-17:

[ταῦτ' ἔδοχσεν τõι δέμοι] ἐπὶ Φ stoichedon 39
[ιλοκράτ]ος ἄρχ[οντ]ος. *vac.*

Whether or not the phrase ταῦτ' ἔδοχσεν τõι δέμοι is "by implication of its position [in a postscript] a proof that the decrees came to the Demos as probouleumata," [6] we may use these postscripts as evidence for the importance of the formula ἔδοχσεν τõι δέμοι, as in i²1, in expressing the legality of the document concerned.

Another enactment formula—this time in its later standard form—is found in i²5 (Sokolowski [1969] 4), regulations for the Eleusinia, dated perhaps *c.* 475-450. [7] This inscription is restored to open thus:

["Εδοχσ]ε̣ν [⁝ τε̃ι βολε̃ι] ⁝ καὶ [τ]õι δέμοι ⁝ hό[τ]ε Παραιβάτε[ς
ἐγραμμάτευε].

There can be no doubting the correctness of the opening supple-

[5] For archon (and secretary) apparently appended as a postscript cf. ii²17, 394/3, vv. 14-15 (see M. J. Osborne, *BSA* lxv 1971, 150-74, especially 156).

[6] Meritt, *art. cit.*, p. 306 note 11.

[7] So D. M. Lewis, according to P. J. Rhodes, *The Athenian Boule*, Oxford, 1972. Woodhead (*S.* xxv 5) prefers a date '*c. med. s.* v.'

ment: καί guarantees that we have here, for the first time,[8] the standard developed form of the enactment formula. We should also note the first appearance of the secretary, the official responsible for the final draft and the inscribing of the document on stone. The form in which he appears to be mentioned is unique: but his presence in the prescript will from this time continue virtually unchallenged.

One further apparent example of the undeveloped form of prescript occurs at a much later date in the fifth century than any of the examples treated so far: i^{2}146 (*S.* xii 36), a proxeny decree for Proxenos, dated *c.* 411/0 by Woodhead.[9] Although Woodhead's attempt to make Proxenos a citizen of the island of Chalke has not found universal assent, no matter what the ethnic restored, the preserved remains indicate a superscript followed by no more than the simple formula of enactment:[10]

Πρόχσενος Χαλκ[ιδέος(?) πρόχσενος καὶ] non-stoichedon
εὐεργέτης Χαλ[--- καὶ οἱ τούτο πα]
ῖδες. *vacat*
[Ἔδ]οχσεν τε͂ι βολε͂ι κα[ὶ το͂ι δέμοι· ἀναγράφσαι Πρ]
[όχσ]ενον τὸν [Χαλ--- ἐστέλει]
[λιθίν]ει ἐν πό[λει κτλ.

---

[8] Excepting, that is, the celebrated decree of Themistokles (ML 23), historically dated 480 but inscribed in the third century. I exclude this document because of the likely contamination from literary sources (e.g. the patronymic and demotic given to Themistokles in v. 3 are certainly not original.)

[9] See *H.* xvii 1948, 57-8.

[10] In a recent paper (*BSA* lxix 1974, 295-8) on i^{2}146 Michael Walbank has managed to read a few more letters and has attempted a restoration based on lines of somewhat greater length. In v. 4 he reads:

[ἔδ]οχσεν τε͂ι βολε͂ι κα[ὶ το͂ι δέμοι· ..c. 9-10.. εἶπεν· ἐπαινέσαι]

which is in itself sufficient to cast grave doubt on his overall reconstruction. For a prescript of the form enactment formula + proposer (Walbank has included the proposer of necessity in order to fill out the extra space created by his other assumptions) is nowhere paralleled. *Faute de mieux*, therefore, I should prefer a text closer to Woodhead's attempt. (Note that, *if* Walbank has correctly deciphered στ]ἐλει at the beginning of v. 6, this can be incorporated into Woodhead's text by rearranging vv. 4-5 thus:

[ἔδ]οχσεν τε͂ι βολε͂ι κα[ὶ το͂ι δέμοι· Πρ]
[όχσ]ενον τὸν [Χαλ---- ἀναγράφσαι]
[ἐστ]ἐλει ἐν πό[λει

It is quite possible therefore that the undeveloped prescript (formula of enactment alone) had a much longer history than the few surviving examples might suggest.

Apart from these few isolated cases, however, the extant material provides clear evidence to support a division of prescripts (for the purpose of description) into two basic types:

Type I: prescript without archon.[11] In this type the following items appear, normally in the order shown

formula of enactment	ἔδοχσεν τε͂ι βολε͂ι καὶ το͂ι δέμοι
name of prytanising tribe	ἡ δεῖνα ἐπρυτάνευε
name of secretary	ὁ δεῖνα ἐγραμμάτευε
name of chairman	ὁ δεῖνα ἐπεστάτε
name of proposer of motion	ὁ δεῖνα εἶπε.[12]

Type II: prescript with archon

formula of enactment	ἔδοχσεν τε͂ι βολε͂ι καὶ το͂ι δέμοι
name of prytanising tribe	ἡ δεῖνα ἐπρυτάνευε
name of secretary	ὁ δεῖνα ἐγραμμάτευε
name of chairman	ὁ δεῖνα ἐπεστάτε
name of archon	ὁ δεῖνα ἔρχε
name of proposer of motion	ὁ δεῖνα εἶπε.[12]

The earliest known example of Type I is perhaps i^{2}16 (ML 31), relations with Phaselis, dated 469-450. The prescript reads as follows: [13]

---

[11] The archon may, of course, appear in the superscript without reappearing in the prescript (see below).

[12] Or equivalent: e.g. the motion may be formulated by ξυγγραφεῖς: cf., e.g., i^{2}22 (BM pp. 35-7), 450/49, τάδε hοι χ]συνγγρα[φε͂ς sic χσυνέγραφσαν; i^{2}76 (ML 73), ?*c*. 422, τάδε οἱ χσυγγραφε͂ς χσυνέ | [γρ]αφσαν; i^{2}109 (D 9), 410/09, [γνόμ]ε το͂ν συνγραφέον; cf. also i^{2}71 (*S*. xii 16), *c*. 436, v. 47, γνόμε] στρατεγο͂ν; ii^{2}27, 416/15, γνώμη στρατηγῶν; and the unique ii^{2}1 (ML 94), 405/4, vv. 6-7, γνώμη Κλεσόφο | καὶ συνπρυτανέον, 'to emphasize that the proposal was unanimous' (ML): the amendment (v. 32) is introduced by the same formula.

[13] I incorporate the improvements to the readings noted by BM (p. 116), though I have reservations about so early an example of ephelkustic nu. (The Ionic lettering is probably an indication that the Phaselites paid for the stone themselves: it has no bearing on the date of the document.)

["Εδο]ξεν τῆι βολῆι καὶ τῶι δ[ή] stoichedon 22
[μωι]· Ἀκαμαντὶ[ς ἐ]πρυτάνευε,
[. . .]σιππος ἐγ[ραμ]μάτευεν, Ἐ
[πιμ]ήδης ἐπεστάτει, Λέω[ν ε]ἶ
[πε·

Among numerous other examples cf., e.g., i^{2}26 (*S*. xii 7), Treaty with the Amphictiony, *c*. 458; i^{2}66 (ML 46), decree of Kleinias, ?447; i^{2}91 (ML 58A), decree of Kallias, 434/3 etc.

Apart, however, from the examples which list the items in the normal order, there is also a secondary sequence: i^{2}27 (*S*. xii 9), a proxeny decree for some Delphians, dated *c*. 450/49, reads thus:

"Εδοχσεν τ[ει βολει καὶ τοι δέ] stoichedon 23
μοι· Λεοντ[ὶς ἐπρυτάνευε, . . .]
όστρατος [ἐπεστάτε, . . . 7 . . .]
ράτες ἐγρ[αμμάτευε, . . . 7 . . .]
χος εἶπε· Ἀ[. . . . 10 . . . . καὶ τὸ]

Here we have a sequence enactment formula, prytanising tribe ----, secretary and proposer. . . . όστρατος must therefore be the epistates.[14] So the secretary and chairman have changed places, conceivably by mere chance,[15] although confirmation of an alternative order[16] is furnished by the proxeny decree i^{2}149 (BM pp. 100-101), dated 430-415. This is a difficult text since it is not clear precisely where the prescript ends and the decree proper begins.[17] Bradeen and McGregor restore thus:

["Εδοχσεν τει βολ]ει κ[αὶ τοι δέμο] stoichedon 25
[ι· . . . εὶς ἐπρυτ]άνευ[ε, . . c. 6 . . ἐπ]
[εστάτε, . . c. 6 . .]ς ἐγρα[μμάτευε, .]
[6 or 8 εἶπε, 3 or 1]υφεμ[2 or 4 καὶ 3 or 1]
[. . . . . . 13 . . . . . .]αιον[. . καλέσα]
[ι κτλ.

---

[14] For whom room must be found.

[15] A cutter whose eye had slipped would be understandably reluctant to begin all over again. And erasure was a messy business.

[16] This alternative order is surely attested in the fourth century: e.g. ii^{2}31 (Tod 117), 386/5.

[17] The sequence of provisions in the decree proper is also unusual. The invitation to entertainment in the prytaneion appears at the beginning and not in its normal position at the end of the decree.

whereas Meritt had read: [18]

[῎Εδοχσεν τε̃ι βολ]ε̃ι κ[αὶ το̃ι δέμο] stoichedon 25
[ι· .ι. εἰ̃ς ἐπρυτ]άνευ[ε . .ᶜ.⁵. . ἐπε]
[στάτε, . . .ᶜ.⁷. . .]ς ἐγρα[μμάτευε, .]
[. . . .⁸. . . . ἔ̃ρχε, Ε]ὔφεμ[ος εἰ̃πε· κα]
[λέσαι μὲν . .⁵. .]αι̃ον [τὸν . .⁵. .]
κτλ.

Whatever the relative merits of the restorations from]υφεμ[on, both these texts were produced on the assumption that it was essential to reduce the space available before ἐγρα[μμάτευε in order to avoid the necessity of furnishing the secretary with a demotic.[19] Patience Haggard had entertained that possibility,[20] but her text will certainly not bear examination. But not necessarily for the reason which troubled Meritt and Bradeen and McGregor.

Meritt [21] accepted the demotic with the name of the secretary in i^{2}47 (*S*. x 136) of 407/6 as the "earliest surely attested use," [22] but doubted the possibility of its appearance in i^{2}72 (*S*. x 88) of *c*. 423/2. He admits that the latter case is "more persuasive" (than i^{2}22) but rejects it in favour of a supposed named archon.

However, since secretaries with demotics are found in superscripts [23] perhaps as early as 450 (*S*. x 15), I find the criterion of 407/6 as a *terminus ante quem non* in prescripts less than convincing. At the very least we should be prepared to entertain the possibility —especially if insistence on the orthodox view leads to further complications—of a secretary with demotic in a document as early as mid-century.

The earliest example of Type II is in the very fragmentary i^{2}19+20 vv. 1-2 (BM pp. 71-2), the alliance with Egesta of 458/7:

stoichedon 48

[Χσυμμαχία καὶ hόρ]χ̣ο[ς] ’Α̣[θ]ε̣ν̣α̣[ίον κα]ὶ ’Εγεσταί[ον]

---

[18] *S*. xii 29 = *H*. xxi 1952, 344-6.

[19] "something unexampled at this period" (BM); "no known instance as early as 417/16" (Meritt).

[20] In her text of *S*. x 105. She allows the epistates to stand at the beginning of v. 4, makes Euphemos the archon, and keeps the proposer to vv. 4-5.

[21] *Art. cit.*, p. 344 note 8.

[22] See also ML 92: ". . . both secretary and *epistates* were given their demotics (ll. 2-3)".

[23] See below pp. 8-9.

[ἔδοχσεν τε͂ι βολε͂ι καὶ τ]ο͂ι [δέμοι· . . .6. . .ὶς] ἐπρυτάνευε, [. .4. .]
[. c. 4. ἐγραμμάτευε, . c. 4.]ο[. .4. .ἐ]π̣[εστάτε, hά]β[ρ]ον ἔρχ̣ε, Ἀρ
[. .4. .]
[. . .εἶπεν· κτλ.

The surviving traces more or less justify the restored sequence of items, and there can be no doubting the presence of the archon, now at least, it seems, vouchsafed to us through the diligence of Bradeen and McGregor.[24] Another early example is i^{2}32 (*S.* x 13), in praise of Sigeion, of 451/0:

Σιγ[ειέον].
[Ἔ]δοχσεν τε͂[ι βολε͂ι καὶ το͂ι δέ] stoichedon 23
[μ]οι· Οἰνε[ὶ]ς [ἐπρυτάνευε, . .4. .]
. ς ἐγραμμάτ[ευε,. . . . .9. . . . ἐ]
πεστάτε, Ἀν[τίδοτος ἔρχε, . 3 .]
[ο]χίδες ε[ἶ]π[εν·

in which Antidotos can be none other than the archon of this year.

Among many other examples of this type cf. i^{2}94 (Sokolowski [1969] 14), on the sanctuary of Kodros, Neleus and Basile, 418/17, almost totally preserved; and i^{2}118 (ML 90), a proxeny decree for Oiniades of Palaiskiathos, 408/7.[25]

There are, however, at least three examples in this period of the archon appearing in the list immediately before the epistates. This is first found in i^{2}105 (ML 91), an honorary decree for Archelaos of Macedon, 407/6. Although considerably restored, there can be little doubting the supplements: [26]

[Ἔδοχσεν τε͂ι βολε͂ι καὶ το͂]ι δέμοι· Ἀκα[μα] stoichedon 31
[ντὶς ἐπρυτάνευε, Φελ]λεὺς [ἐγρ]αμ[μ]άτ[ευ]
[ε, Ἀντιγένες ἔρχε, Σιβ]ύρτιο[ς ἐ]πεστά[τε],
[Ἀλκιβιάδες εἶπε·

For the same order cf. ii^{2}1 vv. 5-7 (ML 94), on the Samians, 405/4;

---

[24] But the controversy still rages: see most recently T.E. Wick, *JHS* xcv 1975, 186-90.

[25] The only completely preserved example of a fifth century proxeny decree.

[26] Even allowing some dispute over *which* archon is involved, we must still assume ὁ δεῖνα ἔρχε in v. 3. Antigenes seems more likely than Wilhelm's Theopompos (411/10).

ii^{2}1 vv. 41-2 and 56-7 (Tod 97),[27] 403/2; ii^{2}16 (Tod 103), alliance with Eretria, 394/3.

One of the commonest features additional to the basic prescripts outlined above is the superscript citation of the secretary's name.[28] The earliest example would appear to be *S*. x 15, treaty with Hermione, dated *c*. 450, where we find the secretary (with demotic) at the head of the stone and his name repeated in the usual position in the prescript:

> [Θε]όδορος Πρασιεὺς ἐγραμμάτευε.
> [Χσ]υνθε̃και ⁝ Ἑρμιονέον ⁝ καὶ Ἀθεναίο[ν].
> [Ἔ]δοχσεν τε̃ι βολε̃ι καὶ τõι δέμοι· Ἀντιοχ[ὶς ἐ] stoichedon 35
> [π]ρυτάνευε, Θεόδορος ἐγραμμάτευε, Σι . . ⁵ . .
> . ἐπεστάτε,
> [Λ]ẹ́ον ε[ἶ]π[ε]·[29]

For other examples of this type cf. i^{2}76 (ML 73), Eleusinian First-fruits, ?*c*. 422; i^{2}144+155 (D23), proxeny decree, ?416/15; ii^{2}2, proxeny decree, 403/2, in all of which the secretary reappears in the prescript without demotic.

The secretary may also be found superscript with patronymic,[30] first in i^{2}57 (ML 65), the Methone decrees, 430-423. This stele was inscribed in 423, when Phainippos was secretary, but it records a series of decrees dating probably from 430 on. The superscript to the whole stone reads:

> Μεθοναίον ἐκ Πιερ[ίας].
> [Φ]αίνιππος Φρυνίχο ἐγραμμάτ[ευε].

and one assumes that in the prescript to the fourth and final decree (which is completely lost) Phainippos would reappear (presumably without patronymic, to judge by the secretaries of prescripts I,

---

[27] The sequence is plain on the stone in the third decree and to be inferred in the second.

[28] For secretaries in superscripts in the period of the Peloponnesian War see H. B. Mattingly, Φόρος, *Tribute to Benjamin Dean Meritt*, 92-3.

[29] Note the vacant space in v. 5 which may have been deliberately left to take the name of the archon.

[30] "A peculiarity of style . . . . in the late 'twenties," B. D. Meritt, *H*. xiv 1945, 111.

II and III).[31] For another example of a secretary with patronymic in a superscript repeated, without patronymic, in the prescript cf. i²81, on bridging the Rheitos at Eleusis, 422/1.[32] i²87 (*S.* x 80), treaty with Halieis, 424/3, shows a superscript with a secretary who must be given either a patronymic or a demotic:

[Νε]οκλείδ[ες . . .⁸ ᵒʳ ⁹. . . ἐγρα]μμάτευε.

He reappears in the prescript with room only for the nomen.

Not infrequently we find the secretary with both patronymic and demotic in a superscript. The first examples appear in 421/0: i²82, proxeny decree for Asteas of Alea:

Προκλέες Ἀτάρβο Εὐον
υμεὺς ἐγραμμάτευε.

In the prescript which follows Prokles reappears with nomen alone. Cf. also i²96 (*S.* x 104), treaty with Argos, 417/16; i²109 (D9), repayment to Athena, 410/09.

The archon [33] too often takes his place beside the secretary in the superscript.[34] The earliest extant example is i²84 (Sokolowski [1969] 13), regulations for the Hephaisteia, of 421/0:

[Θ]ε[οί]
[Προκλε͂ς] Ἀτάρβο Ε[ὐονυμεὺς]
[ἐγραμμάτ]ευε· ἐπὶ Ἀρισ[τίονος ἄρχοντος].
[Ἔδοχσε τε͂ι βολε͂ι καὶ τõι δ]έμοι· hιπποθοντὶ[ς ἐπρυτάνευε, Προκλε͂ς ἐγραμμά] stoichedon 61
[τευε, ... ἐπεστάτε, Ἀρισ]τίον ἐ͂ρχε, hυπέ[ρβολος εἶπε - - -

[31] Cf. i²68 + 69 (BM pp. 88-9), on the Boiotian exiles, 424/3, where [Φιλέα]ς Λύκο [ἐγραμμάτευε] of the superscript is repeated, without patronymic, in the second decree (v. 26).

[32] For the relation between the conciliar year for which Prepis was first secretary and the archon year of Aristion see B. D. Meritt, *Proc. Amer. Philos. Soc.*, cxv 1971, 107-8.

[33] For archons in superscripts see H. B. Mattingly, Φόρος, *Tribute to Benjamin Dean Meritt*, 101-2 (Table A). (Note that under the year 407/6, archon Antigenes, Mattingly's entry in the third column should read 'S+A').

[34] Cf. ii²17, 394/3, vv. 13-15, where both the secretary (with patronymic and demotic) and archon (with demotic) appear as a *postscript* to a decree of the boule (see M. J. Osborne, *art. cit.* [note 5 above]). The secretary has already appeared (nomen alone) in vv. 1-2.

an example notable for the *form* of the archon item in the superscript where it appears as a prepositional phrase.[35] In its repetition in the prescript it takes the form normal in this period, ὁ δεῖνα ἔρχε,[36] a form which seems to be the more usual in superscripts also: cf., e.g., i^{2}115 (ML 86), the law-code of Draco, 409/8:

Διόγν[ε]τος Φρεάρριος ἐγραμμάτε[υε].
Διοκλε͂ς ἔρχε.

In this text the archon does not reappear in the prescript, though Diognetos is present, without demotic. For other examples of this formulation cf. i^{2}119, a proxeny decree, 408/7 (secretary and archon both repeated in prescript); ii^{2}10, citizenship decree, 401/400 (secretary repeated). Another interesting example of the combination is i^{2}124, 406/5, of which only the superscript survives:[37]

['Ερ]ωτίων ἐγραμμάτευεν 'Ελ[ευ]
[σί]νιος.
[Κ]αλλίας 'Αγγελῆθεν ἦρχεν.

Both secretary and archon are given demotics, the secretary having the additional distinction of an idiosyncratic word-order: name-verb-demotic.[38]

In two instances the secretary has yielded primacy to the archon: i^{2}110 (ML 85), honours for Phrynichos' assassins, 410/09):

[ἐπὶ Γλαυκί]ππο ἄ[ρ]χον[τ]ος.
[Λόβον ἐκ] Κεδο͂ν ἐγραμμάτευε.

where both archon (in the form ὁ δεῖνα ἔρχε) and secretary (without demotic) reappear in the prescript; and ii^{2}13, proxeny decree, 399/8:

---

[35] Later *de rigueur* in prescripts. Cf. i^{2}110 (ML 85), 410/09 below.

[36] This differentiation between the form of the prescript and the superscript serves to illustrate the greater freedom exercised by the secretary in drafting the latter. Here he felt free to embellish his text as he saw fit: and it is perhaps no accident of chance that he often chose to give prominence to his own name. Names of secretaries appear noticeably earlier in superscripts than names of archons.

[37] I quote according to BM p. 126.

[38] It is interesting to note that this word-order is extremely common in the Tribute Lists: cf., e.g., List 4 (451/0): ἐπὶ τε͂ς ἀρχε͂ς τε͂ς τετά[ρτ]ες ḥ[ε͂ι . . . ? . . .]-λες ἐγραμμά[τευε hα]λιμόσιος. Cf. also Lists 5 (450/49); 7 (448/7); 8 (447/6); 12 (443/2); but contrast List 11 (444/3), hε͂ι Στρόμ[βιχος Χο]λλείδες ἐγ[ραμ]-μάτευε (so too Lists 13 (442/1) and 15 (440/39). Cf. M. J. Walbank, *H.* xliv 1975, 438-9, footnote 5.

['Αριστο]κράτης ἦρχ[ε].
[Λυσίμαχος Κ]ολωνῆθεν ἐγραμμάτευε.
['Αρισ]τέο Αἰγιῶς.

where only the secretary reappears in the prescript (without demotic).

A third example may be found in the tiny fragment ii^{2}11, 400/399. In the *Corpus* this text reads:

. . . μο -
['Ε]πὶ Λάχη[τος ἄρχοντος -]
.ο 'Αλαιεὺ[ς ἐγραμμάτευε, - - - ις ἐπρυτάνευε.]
[ἔ]δοξεν [τ -]
.τιμ -

This can perhaps be better arranged by making v. 1 contain the name of the person/state involved in the decree; vv. 2-3 as the heading; and vv. 4ff. as the prescript. Thus:

. . . μο -
['Ε]πὶ Λάχη[τος ἄρχοντος, *nomen*, *patronymicum*]
.ο 'Αλαιεὺ[ς ἐγραμμάτευε].
[ἔ]δοξεν [τῆι βουλῆι καὶ τῶι δήμωι· - - - ἐπρυτάνευε κτλ.]

The patronymic ending in -ο (= ου) need not trouble us: a mixture of Attic and Ionic orthography is common enough at this date. .τιμ will presumably be part of the name of the secretary.

In two examples we find a superscript with an archon but no secretary:

(1) i^{2}125, proxeny decree, 405/4: [39]

'Αλεξίας ἦ[ρχεν].
[Π]όλυπος Μενεσθέως [Γορτύνιος?]
[πρ]όξενος καὶ εὐεργέτη[ς 'Αθηναίων].

stoichedon 38

["Εδοξε]ν τῆι βολῆι καὶ τῶ[ι δήμωι· . . . ηὶς ἐπρυτάν]
[ευε, Πο]λυάρατος Χολαργ[εὺς ἐγραμμάτευε, . . ^{5} . .]
[. . . 'Αρ]αφήνιος ἐπεστά[τε, ... ^{8} . . . . εἶπεν·

I quote this text to the end of the prescript in order to illustrate one further point: not only does the secretary appear in the prescript

[39] I incorporate the corrections of BM p. 126.

with a demotic, so too does the epistates for the first time.[40] This latter feature is well paralleled by another document of approximately the same date, ii²1 (ML 94), honours for the Samians, dated to the archonship of Alexias, 405/4, but inscribed (or reinscribed) when Kephisophon was secretary, i.e. in 403/2. In the prescript we read (vv. 5-7):

stoichedon 57-61

Ἔδοχσεν τῆι βολῆι καὶ τῶι δήμωι· Κεκροπὶς ἐπρυτάνευε, Πόλυμνις Εὐωνυμεὺς
ἐγραμμάτευε, Ἀλεξίας ἦρχε, Νικοφῶν Ἀθμονεὺς ἐπεστάτει· γνώμη Κλεσόφο
καὶ συνπρυτάνεον·

And likewise in the prescripts of the two other decrees (of 403/2) which appear later on the stone [41] we read, vv. 41-2:

[ἔδοξεν τῆι βολῆι καὶ τῶι δήμωι· Πανδ]ιονὶς ἐπρυτάνευε, Ἀγύρριος Κ[ολλυτ]εὺς
[ἐγραμμάτευε, Εὐκλείδης ἦρχε, Κα]λλίας Ὤαθεν ἐπεστάτει· Κηφισοφῶν [εἶπεν]·

and vv. 56-7

[ἔδοξεν τῆι βολῆ]ι καὶ τῶι δήμωι· Ἐρεχθηῒς ἐπρυτάνευεν, Κηφισοφῶν Πα[ια]νιεύ[ς]
[ἐγραμμάτευε, Εὐκλ]είδης ἦρχε, Πύθων ἐκ Κηδῶν ἐπεστάτει, Εὐ[- - - εἶπεν·].

(2) ii²12 (ML 80), vv. 29-32, honorary decree, 399/8. Here we find ἐπὶ Ἀριστοκράτος ἄ[ρχοντος] centred in a line by itself before the prescript.

Our review of the material from the fifth century is now virtually complete, but before drawing this chapter to a close I wish first to consider certain texts which show unusual or problematical features:

---

[40] Although a slightly earlier appearance is likely to occur in i²47 (*S.* x 136) (see p. 6 above), where the stone gives a demotic for the secretary and the 15 letter spaces before]ς ἐπεσ[τάτε certainly leave room for a *demoticum*. The document is dated to the first half of 406 in ML 92.

[41] See ii²1.

(1) i^{2}39 (ML 52), relations with Chalkis, 446/5. The prescript reads as follows:

῎Εδοχσεν τε͂[ι β]ολε͂ι καὶ το͂ι δέμοι· ᾽Αντιοχὶς ἐ[πρυτ]
άνευε, Δρακ[ον]τίδες ἐπεστάτε, Διόγνετος εἶπε·

and one is immediately surprised to find no mention of the secretary. It is clear, however, from cuttings on the stone that a second stone was attached on the left and that these two were surmounted by a third. This third stone probably carried a relief and unquestionably bore the name of the secretary, thus suitably emphasised. It is noteworthy that his name does *not* reappear in the prescript, but, as we have seen above, repetition, though common, was not invariable.

(2) i^{2}78 (Sokolowski [1962] 8), regulations for the cult of Apollo, *c.* 430. In this document alone we find the prytanising tribe isolated in the superscript and not repeated in the prescript:

. . ⁵ . . ὶ ς ἐ π ρ υ τ ά ν ε υ ε.
stoichedon 42
[῎Εδοχσεν τε͂ι β]ολε͂ι καὶ το͂ι δέμοι· ᾽Αντικρατίδες ἐγ[ρα]
[μμάτευε, . . ⁵ . .]ος ἐπεστάτε, Φιλόχσενος εἶπε·

The reason for the prominence thus given to the prytanising tribe is not at all evident, and the only text remotely parallel seems to be i^{2}109 (D9), repayment to Athena, 410/09, where the superscript has been restored to read:

[Φ]ίλιππος [Φιλ]έο Δ[ειραδιότες] stoichedon
[ἐ]γραμμάτευεν Οἰ[νεΐδι φυλε͂ι].

a formulation unique in our experience. One is tempted to revert to the text of the *Corpus*, in which . . . εοδ - - - are clearly to be taken as part of the patronymic and Οἰ[as the beginning of a demotic (Οἰναῖος). The word-order with the verb intervening before the demotic has already been commented on above.[42] Meiggs and Lewis,[43] however, argue for an upper stone carrying "a relief and the name of the prytany and the secretary" in order to explain the disputed fragmentary opening of i^{2}24 (ML 44), on the priestess and temple of Nike, ?450-445:

---

[42] See p. 10 above.

[43] P. 111. Meritt (*ATL*) had argued that the main decree was inscribed on an upper stone and that the lower stone which survives carried only amendments.

[. . . . . .18. . . . . τõ]ι̣ [δέ]μο̣[ι . . .] stoichedon 29
[. . . . . . . .17. . . . .]α̣ι̣κος εἶπε·

where there seems room only for the epistates between the end of the enactment formula and the name of the proposer. If this suggestion can be accepted, the appearance of ὁ δεῖνα ἐπρυτάνευε in a superscript will be a parallel for i^{2}78.

(3) i^{2}96 (*S.* x 104), treaty with Argos, 417/16. This document offers a text which apparently has no mover:

. .όδορος Πολυχάρος 'Α[μφιτροπῆθεν(?) ἐγραμμάτευεν]
[Ἔδοχσεν τει] βολει καὶ τõι δέμοι· Αἰαν[τὶς ἐπρυτάνευε, . .όδορος ἐγραμμάτευε],
stoichedon 76
[. . . .10. . . . ἐπεσ]τάτε, Εὔφεμος ἔρχε· χσυ[μμαχίαν καὶ χσυνθέκας ἀδόλος καὶ ἀβλαβες ἔναι 'Αθενα]
[ίοις κτλ.

This is not at all likely, and quite unnecessary. One may read, for example:

Εὔφεμος ἔρχε, Χσύ[μμαχος? εἶπε· χσυμμαχίαν ἔναι ἄδολον καὶ ἀβλαβε 'Αθενα] [44]

The fact that the proposer of a χσυμμαχία bears the name Χσύμμαχος should occasion no more surprise than that the recipient of a προξενία should be called Πρόχσενος.[45]

(4) ii^{2}12 (ML 80), honorary decree for Pythophanes of Karystos, dated to the year 411. Meiggs and Lewis offer the following text:

[. . . .8. . . .]ην[. . . . . .20. . . . .] stoichedon 30
[. . .6. . .]ηι ην τε[. . . . . .18. . . . .]
[. . .6. . .]άτης 'Ικα̣[ριεὺς ἐγραμμάτευεν].
[βολῆ]ς ἐπεστάτε[. . . . . . . .17. . . . .]
[. . .κ]αὶ μετ' αὐτõ π[. . . . . . . .16. . . . .]
[.Ξυ]πεταιών, Διωπ[. . . . . . . .16. . . . .]
[. .]Κεφαλῆθεν, Καλ[. . . . . . . .16. . . . .]
[.'Ι]ππομένης εἶπε·[

In the decree which follows (vv. 8-28) it is resolved to inscribe a previous decree in honour of Pythophanes, a decree which pre-

[44] So the footnote in *S.* x 104.
[45] i^{2}146 (*S.* xii 36).

sumably was cut higher on the stone. (Meiggs and Lewis suggest that this decree may end in vv. 1-2). At vv. 29-32 we have the beginning of a third decree [46] (of 399/8), presumably also in honour of Pythophanes.

On their assumption that the surviving decree began at v. 3 Meiggs and Lewis find restoration of the prescript not a little troublesome: "the prescript ... has no epigraphical parallel whatsoever," they claim. Lewis, rather desperately, attempted a reading (vv. 1-2) [ἔδοξεν] | [τῆι βολ]ῆι· ἧν τε[τάρτη τῆς πρυτανείας, in an effort to reconcile it with the other known decree of the period, Plut. *Vit. X Orat.* 833d ἔδοξεν τῇ βουλῇ, μιᾷ καὶ εἰκοστῇ τῆς πρυτανείας· Δημόνικος Ἀλωπεκῆθεν ἐγραμμάτευε, Φιλόστρατος Παλληνεὺς ἐπεστάτει, Ἄνδρων εἶπε. But such a restoration will hardly commend itself: it is totally unparalleled and syntactically dubious. Nor should we pay too much attention to the form of decrees preserved only in a literary tradition.

Clearly, as Wilhelm pointed out, there is space for five names in vv. 4-7, and these have been connected with the five proedroi of the Four Hundred (Thuc. 8.67.3) and with the constitution described in Arist. *Ath. Pol.* 30.4. However that may be, the form of the prescript underlying these fragmentary lines is quite different from anything else we possess and can hardly be recovered unless some further fragment of this section is rediscovered.[47]

Finally, a word about a series of documents from the early fourth century [48] which carry not the customary enactment formula ἔδοξεν τῆι βουλῆι καὶ τῶι δήμωι but simply ἔδοξεν τῆι βουλῆι, thus apparently indicating conciliar origin alone. These are mainly proxeny decrees: ii²6 (Tod 98), *c.* 400; ii²12 (ML 80), vv. 29-32, 399/8; ii²13, 399/8; *H.* vii 91-2, 11, *c.* 398-390; ii²32, 385/4; ii²49, ?*paullo post* 385/4 [49]; ii²63, *ante* 378/7; ii²77, *ante* 378/7; ii²95, 377/6; also a citizenship award, ii²17, 394/3. The question is: does

---

[46] In a different 'hand.'

[47] Perhaps it is worth considering the possibility that Ἱ]ππομένης εἶπε introduces an *amendment* (without the normal formula τὰ μὲν ἄλλα καθάπερ: cf. i²24 (ML 44), v. 14). This would remove any need to cast vv. 2 (or 3)-8 in the form of a prescript.

[48] Some of the texts adduced here are in fact later than 394/3, the lower limit of the present chapter. They are, however, most conveniently dealt with at this point.

[49] See *S.* xxi 224.

this evidence suggest that, for a short time after the restoration of the democracy, the boule acquired powers normally reserved for the ecclesia? Or can some other explanation be found?

Rhodes [50] suggests two ways in which we may account for these documents: (i) the boule was merely authorising the publication [51] (or republication of damaged or destroyed stones) of honours already conferred by the ecclesia. As an example one may quote ii^{2}6, where the boule directs the secretary to renew a stele destroyed under the Thirty; cf. ii^{2}17, a decision of the boule to inscribe a decree of the people which appears later on the stone;
(ii) some of these documents may in fact be probouleumata ratified by the ecclesia, but drafted for inscribing by the secretary with the wrong enactment formula (taken from the records of the boule). This must certainly be the explanation of ii^{2}16 (Tod 103), the treaty with Eretria, where it is inconceivable that the people delegated such authority to the boule.

In one case, ii^{2}32, both explanations are applicable. At vv. 19 ff. we have an amendment in the form τὰ μ]ὲν [ἄλ] | [λα] καθάπερ τῆι βο[λῆι, which guarantees ratification of the motion by the ecclesia; and, although the inscription is dated (by the archon in the superscript) to 385/4, the reference to the possibility of the honorand being unjustly treated ἐν τῶμ πόλε[ων ὅσων 'Α]θην[αῖοι κρατ]ῶσ[ι]ν is a clear indication that the decree refers to a time 'valente etiamtum Atheniensium imperio.' [52]

ii^{2}77, *ante* 378/7, perhaps deserves individual consideration. Here the enactment formula is expressed in both decrees, vv. 1-2 and 9-10, in the form ἔδοξεν τῆι βουλῆι κατὰ τὸ τοῦ δήμου ψήφισμα. Vv. 5-8 show that decree I is ordering publication of decree II. Decree I thus falls under explanation (i), and it may well be that in the second decree the enactment formula has simply been erroneously and mechanically repeated from the first.

Clearly we cannot always be certain which explanation to apply, but it does seem that we have every justification to have recourse to one (or both) of them in dealing with texts of this nature.[53]

---

[50] I am greatly indebted to Rhodes' discussion of these texts (*op. cit.*, pp. 83-5).

[51] Admittedly ii^{2}172, *ante* 353/2 is a case in point where the boule *did* refer decision on a matter of mere publication to the people.

[52] See the note in the *Corpus*.

[53] R. A. de Laix, however, (*Probouleusis at Athens*, pp. 125-6 and 138)

Two other texts remain to be considered here:

(1) ii²18 (Tod 108), an honorary decree for Dionysios of Syracuse, 394/3. This too displays the enactment formula ἔδοξεν τῆι βολῆι but, as Rhodes argues (*pace* Tod), a head of state would normally be praised by the demos or not at all, and honours conferred by a lesser body would not be published unless accompanied by those of the demos also. We can therefore conclude that this fragment is either incorrectly labelled or is an independent decree of the boule below which a decree of the demos was also inscribed.

(2) ii²145, which contains two decrees: in the first of these Eukles is appointed herald of the boule and demos (*c.* 398-390), and in the second his son, Philokles, is appointed to the same position (*c.* 368-353). The second decree carries the normal enactment formula [ἔδοξεν τῆι βολῆι καὶ] τῶι δήμωι,[54] but the first is restored to read only [ἔδοξεν τῆι βολῆι].[55] We can agree with Rhodes in finding it not a little strange that the boule will thus have had the power to make the father's appointment but not the son's without recourse to the people. We should therefore read [ἔδοξεν τῶι δήμωι] and so remove this text from among such apparent decisions of the boule.[56]

It is outwith the scope of this study to discuss in detail the significance of the distinction between the two enactment formulae which are found in use for decrees of the demos from 403/2 onwards. We may recall that in the very earliest texts the enactment formula was ἔδοχσεν τõι δέμοι: this was replaced by ἔδοχσεν τε̃ι βολε̃ι καὶ τõι δέμοι as the standard formula for all decrees of the demos until very near the end of the fifth century. At this point we find both ἔδοξεν τῆι βουλῆι καὶ τῶι δήμωι and ἔδοξεν τῶι δήμωι.[57]

---

is more inclined to accept this series of documents as evidence for the boule acting independently of the ecclesia. But his comments do not carry conviction.

[54] The restoration is guaranteed by the stoichedon pattern.

[55] D. M. Lewis, *BSA* xlix 1954, 36-7.

[56] One's judgement here will, of course, be affected by one's opinion of the case for increased powers for the boule in the early years of the fourth century. I have tried to show, however, that certainly in the matter of proxeny decrees, there is no support for such a thesis.

[57] ἔδοξεν τῶι δήμωι is restored in ii²3, a proxeny decree dated *c.* 400. Cf. the decree *apud* Andocides, i.83, of 403/2.

Rhodes [58] attempts to demonstrate that the difference between the two formulae reflects a difference in procedure: that from this time the Athenians (or their secretaries) decided that it would be convenient to differentiate probouleumata ratified *verbatim* in the ecclesia from all other enactments of the demos (whether revised from a probouleuma, or framed in response to an 'open' probouleuma, or resolved contrary to the wishes of the boule). Secretaries, however, were careless—or at least inconsistent—in the application of the appropriate formula, and, moreover, during the first half of the fourth century there was still a tendency to apply the formula ἔδοξεν τῆι βουλῆι καὶ τῶι δήμωι to any enactment of the demos, whether appropriate or not.[59]

What concerns this study, however, is not so much which formula of enactment is chosen but in which position it appears in the prescript sequence. It is on this aspect of the enactment formula that I shall henceforth concentrate.

---

[58] *Op. cit.*, pp. 66-78.

[59] In discussing the imprecise application of enactment formulae in the fourth century de Laix argues for the incompetence of secretaries now appointed by lot (although he sees the move to annual secretaries as one calculated to produce greater efficiency in the performance of secretarial duties, *op. cit.*, p. 77). Rhodes (*JHS* xciv 1974, 233) correctly points out that the fourth century was a period of transition (not of chaos) between the single formulaic pattern of the fifth century and the two alternative patterns of later Athens.

CHAPTER TWO

THE FIRST HALF OF THE FOURTH CENTURY [1]

In the first chapter we have seen the Athenian documentary prescript begin to take shape: we have witnessed the gradual sophistication and the manifold experimentation with different forms and combinations of the items of information which, by the end of the fifth century, were clearly felt to be essential ingredients in the prescription—the formula of enactment, the names of the prytanising tribe, of the secretary of the prytany, of the epistates of the day, and of the proposer of the motion (or 'orator', as he is frequently referred to). In many instances too the name of the archon is included in this list.

In the first half of the fourth century the picture is, predictably, one of continuing refinement of detail, in particular in the matter of precision in the dating of the document to hand. Amongst the earliest decrees we examined we found dating by archon-year (the Hecatompedon inscriptions of 485/4), but for the decrees of approximately the second half of the fifth century such indication of date as is given tends to be in terms of the tribe in prytany and of the secretary of that prytany. Neither of these items is in itself a very clear indication either of the year or of a point within the year, since (at this period) the secretary held office for only one prytany [2] and so only the *first* secretary of the boule was a meaningful time-indicator, and since the order of the tribes in prytany was

---

[1] There are only some 50 prescripts sufficiently preserved to serve as a basis of study for this period (approximately 394-349). It should be noted that I have *not* taken into account the prescripts of the few inscribed νόμοι from the fourth century. These prescripts are modelled on those of ψηφίσματα but do not include reference to the boule or ecclesia. (This may or may not constitute evidence that these two bodies were excluded from the process of νομοθεσία). For the procedure involved in the enactment of νόμοι see Rhodes, *op. cit.*, 49-52 and Table H (p. 276), and cf. de Laix, *op. cit.*, 52-68 and 135-6. For a recently published νόμος of the year 375/4 see Ronald S. Stroud, *H.* xliii 1974, 157-188, especially 162-3.

[2] So probably until 366/5, when the secretary became elected by lot from outside the bouleutae and held a term of office for one year: see Dinsmoor, *AA* p. 351.

determined by lot and could therefore be ascertained only by consulting the state records.[3]

Of course, many documents continued to mention the archon (as e.g. i^{2}19+20 vv. 1-2 (ML 37), 458/7), thus clearly pointing to the year in question, although there is some reason to believe that archon references are not particularly numerous much before the last quarter of the century.[4]

These two methods of dating (by archon and by prytany) reflect the double calendaric system that obtained in Athens: the festival (or archontic) calendar [5] and the civil (or bouleutic) calendar.[6] Obviously the bouleutic calendar was the more appropriate and the more convenient for the purpose of placing resolutions at a precise point within the chronological framework of the enacting body. And although in course of time the day of enactment came to be given in terms of both calendars (day of lunar month + day of conciliar prytany), the evidence of the early fourth century demonstrates clearly the greater significance of the bouleutic date. For the tribe in prytany is first given its ordinal number in prescripts of the 390s, and a count of days within the prytany is established by the 360s, whereas we have no reference to the day of the lunar month until the 340s.

It will then be the purpose of this chapter to show how this increased concern with the dating of documents is evidenced by the prescripts. I shall begin by considering the increased prominence of the archon, prominence, that is, in frequency and primacy of position. The archon provides the year, the widest chronological context in which further details can specify the section of the year and even the very day of the year on which a resolution was carried.

A. *The archon*

(1) Archon in superscripts: In chapter I we noticed how the archon frequently accompanies the secretary in the superscripts of decrees. An analysis of the evidence for 394-349 will show

[3] See Dinsmoor, *op. cit.*, p. 349.

[4] I have, however, emphasised the paucity of material on which this judgement is based. Archon dates from the *middle* of the century are certainly not to be ruled out on principle.

[5] I.e. the religious calendar, divided into lunar months, by which all the many festivals were fixed; and, incidentally, by which the ordinary citizen reckoned.

[6] I.e. the conciliar calendar, divided into prytanies, the tribal subdivisions of the boule which took it in turn to act as a standing committee of that body.

that the archon came to oust the secretary from this position of emphasis at the head of a stone.

a) Secretary without archon: In only 6[7] certain instances does the secretary appear alone in the superscript; in only 4 of these (the first four)[8] does the archon not make an appearance in the following prescript. In ii^{2}96 the archon appears at the very beginning of the prescript ([ἐ]πὶ Ἱπποδάμαν[τος ἄρχοντος), and in Tod 137 as the last item before the orator (Π]ολύζηλος [ἦρχ]ε).

In one further instance of much later date, ii^{2}127 (Tod 157), 356/5, we find the secretary alone at the top of the stone:

[Γ]ραμματεὺς Λυσίας Λυσ[...... Πιθεύς].
Συμμαχία Ἀθηναίων πρὸς Κετρίπορ[ιν τὸν Θρᾶικα καὶ το]
ὺς ἀδελφοὺς καὶ πρὸς Λύππειον τὸν [Παίονα καὶ πρὸς Γρά]
βον τὸν Ἰλλυριόν.

The date of this document may well have a bearing on the unparalleled splendour of the secretary's designation: 356/5 was the very year in which was inaugurated the use of the official order of the tribes in the appointment of prytany secretaries.[9] I suggest, therefore, that, in this document of the eleventh day of the *first* prytany of the year (i.e. presumably one of the earliest enactments under the new system) the secretary celebrated the event in his own way by prominently displaying his name[10] in an unusual formulation. But by the ninth prytany of the same year he had reverted to the style which gave the archon pride of place (see ii^{2}128 (Tod 159); and cf. ii^{2}129).[11]

---

[7] ii^{2}26, between 394 and 387; ii^{2}49, *paullo post* 385/4; ii^{2}58, *ante* 378/7; ii^{2}77, *ante* 378/7; ii^{2}96 (Tod 126), 375/4; and Tod 137, 367/6. Also possibly in ii^{2}59, *ante* 378/7. Note that ii^{2}58 shows the sequence name-verb-demotic (discussed above p. 10). ii^{2}59 is almost certainly to be restored along the same lines, thus:

[θ] ε [ο ί]
[Πο]λυκλῆ[ς ἐγραμμάτευεν] stoichedon
[Φιλ]αΐδης. *vacat.*

[8] I.e. apparently the four earliest examples, according to the dates indicated in the *Corpus*.

[9] Beginning with Tribe VII (perhaps chosen by lot): see Dinsmoor, *op. cit.*, p. 354.

[10] With demotic, of course, to confirm his tribal affiliation (VII).

[11] It is significant that ii^{2}127 is also the latest example of a secretary in a superscript. At a much later date, however, anagrapheis are found once more in this position of prominence (see Chapter IV below).

b) Secretary and archon: This combination appears to occur in only a few instances, in only one of which does the name of the secretary *precede* that of the archon: ii^{2}44 (Tod 124), 378/7:

[᾿Αρ]ιστοτέλης :·: Εὐφιλήτο stoichedon
[᾿Αχ]αρνεὺς ἐγραμμάτευε[ν]
[᾿Επ]ὶ Ναυσινίκο ἄρχοντος.

In the other examples the archon comes first: in old style, ὁ δεῖνα ἦρχε, in ii^{2}28 (Tod 114), 387/6; in new style, ἐπὶ τοῦ δεῖνος ἄρχοντος, in ii^{2}32, 385/4:

᾿Επὶ Δεξ[ιθέο ἄρχοντος].
Φιλόξεν[ος ἐγραμμάτευε].

where, however, the secretary seems to redress the balance by re-appearing in a unique *postscript*, separated by an uninscribed line from the end of the decree:

[Φιλόξ]ενο[ς Δ]ημαινέτο [Θορ]ίκιος
[ἐγραμ]μ[ά]τ[ευ]ε.

and in ii^{2}43 (Tod 123), the Charter of the Second Athenian Confederacy, 378/7, a document of great interest both intrinsically and formally:

᾿Επὶ Ναυσινίκο ἄρχοντος.
vacat 0.088
Καλλίβιος ⋮ Κηφισοφῶντος
Παιανιεὺς ⋮ ἐγραμμάτευεν.
vacat 0.19
᾿Επὶ τῆς ῾Ιπποθωντίδο[ς ἑβδ]όμης πρυτα
νείας· ἔδοξεν τῆι βολ[ῆι κα]ὶ τῶι δήμω
ι, Χαρῖνος ᾿Αθμον[εὺς ἐπ]εστάτει·
᾿Αριστοτέλης εἶ[πεν·

Although the appearance of this heading is one of a superscript (vv. 1-6) in larger letters followed by the orator in v. 7 (or of a superscript, vv. 1-3, followed by a divided prescript, vv. 4-7), in reality vv. 1-7 *in their entirety* function as a prescript, albeit of unusual shape and sequence.[12]

[12] The explanation of the imposing form of vv. 1-6 may again lie in the importance of the document being inscribed.

Cf. also ii²101, 373/2, an honorary decree of which only the superscript survives:

'Επὶ 'Αστείο ἄρχοντος. non-stoichedon
'Αλκέτο τοῦ Λεπτίνο Συρακοσίο.
'Ακαμαντὶς ἐπρυτάνευε,
Θουδαίτης Διομειεὺς ἐγραμμάτε[υε].

c) Archon without secretary: There are 6 examples of the archon occupying first position on the stone.[13] Cf. also ii²110 (Tod 143), 363/2, where ἐπὶ Χαρικλείδου ἄρχοντος ἐπὶ | τῆς Οἰνηΐδος ἕκτης πρυτανείας appears immediately after the heading giving the name of the euergetes, and ii²136, 354/3, where ἐπὶ Διοτ[ίμου ἄρχοντος] follows straight upon the name of the proxenos honoured.

The evidence of the superscripts is therefore plain: there is a strong tendency to emphasise the position of the archon, not, of course, to gratify that official's pride, but to give a clear and immediate indication of the *year* in which the resolution was passed.

(2) Archon in prescripts:[14]

a) Old style:

(i) Archon absent from both superscript and prescript: ii²26, between 394 and 387; ii²58, *ante* 378/7; ii²77, *ante* 378/7; ii²152, *ante* 370; ii² 207, 349/8.

(ii) Archon in superscript but not in prescript: ii²31 (Tod 117), 386/5; ii²112 (Tod 144), 362/1; ii²114 (Tod 146), 362/1; ii²116 (Tod 147), 361/0.[15]

(iii) Archon in superscript and prescript: ii²28 (Tod 114), 387/6; ii²136, 354/3.

(iv) Archon in prescript but not in superscript: ii²23, 388/7; Tod 137, 367/6; ii²206, 349/8. Cf. also ii²107 (Tod 131), 368/7:

---

[13] ii²31 (Tod 117), 386/5; ii²112 (Tod 144), 362/1; ii²114 (Tod 146), 362/1; ii²116 (Tod 147), 361/0; ii²128 (Tod 159), 356/5; and ii²129, 356/5, which is the latest known example of a superscript archon, apart from ii²406 with which it could just conceivably join. However, the information supplied in the *Corpus* does not seem to favour such a union.

[14] For ease of reference I use the term 'old style' for that style in which the items are listed in a series in the form ὁ δεῖνα + imperfect indicative (so ὁ δεῖνα ἦρχεν); and the term 'new style' for that style in which the more sophisticated syntax introduced by ἐπὶ τοῦ δεῖνος ἄρχοντος appears.

[15] (i) and (ii) taken together suggest that by *c.* 370 it was felt that the archon must appear either superscript or in the prescript. ii²207 may be explained, I suspect, by assuming the loss of a superscript containing mention of the archon.

[θ]εοί.
[Μυτ]ιληναίων.
[Ναυσιγ]ένης ἦρχεν, Αἰαντὶς ἐπρυ — stoichedon 26
[τάνευε]ν, Μόσχος Κυδαθηναιεὺς ἐ
[γραμμά]τευεν, Ἀρίστυλλος Ἐρχι[ε]
[ὺς ἐπεσ]τάτει. *vacat*
vacat 0.215 — non-stoichedon
[ἔδο]ξεν τῆι βουλῆι καὶ τῶι δήμωι· *vacat*
[Διό]φ[αντος ε]ἶπεν·

where again, contrary to appearances, the superscript actually ends in v. 2. The archon therefore appears, old style, in a prescript disguised as a superscript.[16]

b) New style: ἐπὶ τοῦ δεῖνος ἄρχοντος in the first position in a prescript is found in ii^{2}18 (Tod 108), 394/3;[17] ii^{2}34 (Tod 118), 384/3; ii^{2}96 (Tod 126), 375/4; ii^{2}99, 375/4; ii^{2}103 (Tod 133), 369/8; ii^{2}104 (Tod 134), 368/7; and, in the curious 'hybrid' form of prescript,[18] ii^{2}106 (Tod 135), 368/7, and ii^{2}108, 366/5.

B. *The tribe in prytany*

Having now completed a survey of the prominence of the archon, the item which gives the document its chronological orientation to a given year, I turn now to the second element of chronological significance, the tribe in prytany.

In the old style formulation ἡ δεῖνα ἐπρυτάνευε could not of itself automatically convey the information as to which section of the year was implied: one had to have recourse to the state records to discover the position held in the sequence of prytanies by that tribe in that particular year. For no ordinal numeral was attached to the name of the prytanising tribe,[19] nor was the order of succession of the tribes laid down in any regular or predetermined fashion but decided by lot prytany by prytany. It is therefore a matter of the greatest significance (and utility) when the ordinal begins

[16] For this type of 'superscript prescript' see below pp. 28-29.

[17] Like ii^{2}107 a superscript in appearance but a prescript in form and function.

[18] To be discussed below, p. 30.

[19] The ordinal does appear much earlier in the case of financial documents e.g. i^{2}295 (ML 61), 433/2, vv. 10-11: [ἐπὶ τε͂ς Αἰαν]τίδος πρυτανείας πρότες πρυ | [τανευόσες; cf. vv. 21-2.

to appear with the prytanising tribe in the prescripts of decrees.

The first example occurs in ii^{2}18 (Tod 108), apparently an enactment of the boule alone,[20] in honour of Dionysios of Syracuse, 394/3:

'Επ' Εὐβολίδο ἄρχοντος ἐπὶ τῆς Π[ανδιο]
νίδος ἕκτης πρυτανευόσης [21] *vacat*
ἧι Πλάτων Νικοχάρος Φλυεὺ[ς ἐγρα]
μμάτευε.
ἔδοξεν τῆι βολῆι· Κινησίας εἶπε· stoichedon 34

Although vv. 1-4 are inscribed in larger letters with the appearance of a superscript, they are clearly enough part and parcel (but prominently set off) of the prescript. And, more important (for our present examination) than the first real appearance of the first three items (archon, prytanising tribe and secretary) in the more sophisticated form of the later prescript, is the ordinal ἕκτης, clearly specifying the position of the prytany within the archon year 394/3.[22]

Ordinal numerals are never joined to the prytanising tribe when it is expressed in the form ἡ δεῖνα ἐπρυτάνευε. Conversely, the ordinal always appears if the formulation is ἐπὶ τῆς --- πρυτανείας: so the appearance of the ordinal and the new style formulation—which increases steadily, especially from the early 360s on—[23] run *pari passu*.

Before leaving the prytany item one unusual formulation warrants individual consideration: ii^{2}114 (Tod 146), 362/1:

---

[20] But see Rhodes, *op. cit.*, p. 84, for an explanation of the enactment fromula.

[21] Interestingly enough, the first appearance of the ordinal is coupled with the participle πρυτανευόσης (rather than the noun πρυτανείας), as in the earliest financial documents showing the same phenomenon.

[22] Rhodes, *op. cit.* p. 226, refers to this example as "first found in heading", but this is not a strictly accurate description. Likewise, ii^{2}43 (Tod 123) is to be classified as a prescript, not a superscript (although from vv. 4-7, as printed in Tod, this is not immediately evident.)

[23] ii^{2}34 (Tod 118), 384/3; ii^{2}43 (Tod 123), 378/7; ii^{2}96 (Tod 126), 375/4; ii^{2}99 and 100, 375/4; ii^{2}103 (Tod 133), 369/8; ii^{2}104 (Tod 134), 368/7; ?ii^{2}105 + 523 (Tod 136), 368/7; ii^{2}106 (Tod 135), 368/7; ii^{2}108, 366/5; ii^{2}109, 363/2; ii^{2}110 (Tod 143), 363/2; ii^{2}115, 362/1; *S.* xvii 19, *c.* 362-355; ii^{2}123 (Tod 156), 357/6; ii^{2}121 and 122, 357/6; ?*H.* xiii 229-231, 3, 357/6; ii^{2}127 (Tod 157), 356/5; ii^{2}128 (Tod 159), 356/5; ii^{2}130 and ?133, 355/4; ?ii^{2}205, 351/0; ii^{2}206, 349/8. (But NOT ii^{2}107 (Tod 131), 368/7; Tod 137, 367/6; ii^{2}111 (Tod 142), 363/2; ii^{2}112 (Tod 144), 362/1.)

['Επὶ] Μόλωνος ἄρχοντος ἐπ[ὶ] τῆς 'Ερεχ[θ]ηΐδο[ς ἐνάτης].

This line is inscribed in larger letters superscript to a decree which then continues in old style. The last word has been restored as the ordinal, and this must certainly be correct, since the space available is insufficient for πρυτανείας.[24] It may well be that the cutter did not calculate the space properly to allow for the size of the letters chosen in v. 1. However, examples from later prescripts, where we find ἐπὶ τῆς - - - ordinal (without πρυτανείας) make it quite possible that such a formulation without the noun had become established as an acceptable, and perfectly intelligible, expression.[25]

Larfeld [26] had seen in the new form of prescript a neatly and logically graduated system of dating: archon/year; tribe in prytany and secretary/month; epistates/day of month. But this is manifestly *too* neat: the secretary—unless, of course, he is the *first* secretary of the year—affords no greater precision of date than the name of the prytany to which he is attached, and later,[27] when his office became annual, the most obvious way to designate a year was still by the eponymous archon. Furthermore, one can hardly claim that the epistates owes his inclusion in the prescript to his usefulness as a means of designating the day of a particular resolution: if this had been the criterion for his inclusion, he would surely have appeared nearer the beginning of the prescript (presumably immediately after the archon and prytanising tribe) and it would not have been felt necessary further to specify the day by introducing mention of the day of the prytany or of the day of the lunar month.[28] It seems rather that the epistates is included simply as the official bearing the responsibility for putting the matter under discussion to the vote.

Nevertheless the need to specify the day did make itself felt, and this leads us to consider the third element introduced in this period as an aid to dating precision.

---

[24] As pointed out by Schoell.

[25] So e.g. ii²218, 346/5: ἐπὶ τῆς 'Ακαμαντίδ|ος ἐνάτης; ii²224, 343/2: ἐπὶ τῆς Αἰγηΐ|δος δεκάτης.

[26] *Handbuch der griechischen Epigraphik*, II.ii, 1902, p. 649.

[27] Probably in 366/5: see Dinsmoor, *AA* p. 351.

[28] Cf. the remarks of F.-X. Druet, *Revue Belge de Philologie et d'Histoire* xlix 1971, 79-80.

C. *The number of the day of the prytany*

The first example occurs (heavily restored) in the fragmentary ii^{2}105+523 (Tod 136), 368/7: [29]

['Επὶ Ναυσιγέν]ος ἄρχ[οντος ἐπὶ τῆς Αἰαντί] stoichedon 33
[δος ἑβδόμης π]ρυταν[είας, Μόσχος Κυδαθην]
[αιεὺς ἐγραμ]μάτευε, [δευτέραι καὶ τριακο]
[στῆι τῆς πρυ]τανεία[ς· τῶν προέδρων ἐπεψή]
[φιζε . . .⁶. . .]ς Δαίππο [Μαραθ·[30] ἔδοξεν τῶι δή]
[μωι· Πάν]δ[ιος] εἶπεν·

Undoubtedly a numeral is to be restored in vv. 3-4.[31]

D. *Prescripts in general*

It is now appropriate to examine the overall form of the prescripts, to show how they developed as a unit in the period under consideration. The example quoted immediately above is typical of the progress being made in the general direction of the later stock prescript. Note the form and sequence of its elements:

archon	ἐπὶ τοῦ δεῖνος ἄρχοντος
prytanising tribe	ἐπὶ τῆς - - - ίδος ordinal πρυτανείας
secretary	(ἧι) ὁ δεῖνα patronymic demotic ἐγραμμάτευε
day of prytany	ordinal τῆς πρυτανείας
chairman	τῶν προέδρων ἐπεψήφιζεν ὁ δεῖνα demotic [32]
enactment formula	
orator	ὁ δεῖνα εἶπεν.

[29] In financial documents reference to the number of the day of the prytany is found as early as i^{2}295 (ML 61), 433/2, vv. 10-12: [ἐπὶ τε͂ς Αἰαν]τίδος πρυτανείας πρότες πρυ|[τανευόσες, τ]ρε͂ς καὶ δέκα ἐμέραι ἐσελελυ|[θυῖαι ἔσαν; vv. 21-3: ἐπὶ τε͂ς] Αἰαντίδος πρυτανείας | [πρότες πρυτανευόσε]ς τε͂ι τελευτ[αίαι ἐμέ]|[ραι τε͂ς πρυτανείας.

[30] For the abbreviation of the demotic cf. e.g., ii^{2}123 (Tod 156), 357/6 v. 6. The phenomenon is by no means unusual in the second half of the fourth century.

[31] τετάρτηι could appear in place of δευτέραι. For other examples of the day of the prytany cf. ii^{2}109, 363/2; *S.* xvii 19, between 362 and 355 (an unusual prescript to be discussed below); ii^{2}116 (Tod 147), 361/0; ii^{2}123 (Tod 156), 357/6; ii^{2}127 (Tod 157), 356/5; ii^{2}130, 355/4; ii^{2}205, 351/0.

[32] By 378/7 the presidency of the boule and ecclesia had passed from the prytaneis to a board of proedroi, comprising one man from each of the tribes not in prytany; one of this board was the epistates for the day. Thus from this time on the epistates named in the prescripts of decrees represents a deme that does not belong to the tribe in prytany. (So, e.g., in ii^{2}43 (Tod 123), 378/7, Χαρῖνος 'Αθμον[εύς is the epistates τῶν προέδρων, not τῶν πρυτά-

The fourth century is a time when the new style of prescript gradually gained ground at the expense of the less complex old style. There was, however, no uniform movement from old to new, but rather a long period of transition and frequent reversions to old style just when one is beginning to feel that the revolution may have been completed.

One element of the prescript is particularly significant in tracing the development of old into new viz. the enactment formula.[33] Traditionally this had stood as the opening item in the prescript, giving the legal sanction to the decree which followed. In the period under examination there is a very interesting series of documents in which this traditional position has been taken into account, even in texts which otherwise betray all the signs of the new style. E.g. ii²18 (Tod 108), 394/3:

'Επ' Εὐβολίδο ἄρχοντος ἐπὶ τῆς Π[ανδιο]
νίδος ἕκτης πρυτανευόσης *vacat*
ῆι Πλάτων Νικοχάρος Φλυεὐ[ς ἐγρα]
μμάτευε·
ἔδοξεν τῆι βολῆι· Κινησίας εἶπε· stoichedon 34

I have previously remarked on the form of this document: vv. 1-4 have the appearance of a superscript but are in fact an integral part of the prescript. Most noteworthy is the position and arrangement of the enactment formula in v. 5: it stands at the beginning of a new line, in such a way that the drafter creates the illusion of an old style prescript opening with the enactment formula, whereas in reality the formula appears in sequence in its *new* position (that is to say usually immediately before the name of the orator).[34]

ii²109, 363/2, is set out in very much the same way:

νεων.) The formula τῶν προέδρων ἐπεψήφιζεν ὁ δεῖνα first appears in ii²44 (Tod 124), 378/7 (cf. ii²103 (Tod 133), 369/8): but the older formulation does not disappear completely until *c.* 340. (For the date of the institution of the proedroi see D. M. Lewis, *BSA* xlix 1954, 31-4; for the reason for their institution see Rhodes, *op. cit.*, pp. 26-7., and in particular J. H. Thiel, 'De Voorzitter van de Atheense Volksvergadering', *Mededelingen der Koninklijke Nederlandse Akademie van Wetenschappen*, afd. Letterkunde, nieuwe reeks, deel 28, no. 8, 1965, 433-441. Cf. also de Laix, *op. cit.*, 75-6.)

[33] Omitted in only one document of this period, ii²104 (Tod 134), 368/7, where there seems no room to restore it. However, as we shall see later, omission in the late third and early second centuries was not uncommon.

[34] For the omission of the epistates in this document see note 47 below.

['Επὶ Χαρ]ικλεἰδο ἄρχοντο[ς ἐπὶ τ] stoichedon 25
[ῆς 'Ακα]μαντίδος δευτέρα[ς πρυτ]
[ανεία]ς ἧι Νικόστρατο[ς Φιλοστ]
[ράτο] Παλληνεὺς ἐγρα[μμάτευεν]·
[τρι]ακοστῆι τῆς πρυτ[ανείας].
[ἔδ]οξεν τῆι βολῆι καὶ τῶι δ[ήμωι·..⁵..] stoichedon 31
...ης Παιανιεὺς ἐπεστάτε[ι, Κρατῖνος?]
[ε]ἶπεν·

Once again, despite appearances, vv. 1-8 are to be classed as a prescript. Note how the enactment formula is so placed as to bear the appearance of opening a prescript.[35]

The same effect is also achieved in ii^{2}107 (Tod 131), 368/7:

[Θ]εοί.
[Μυτ]ιληναίων.
[Ναυσιγ]ένης ἦρχεν, Αἰαντὶς ἐπρυ stoichedon 26
[τάνευε]ν, Μόσχος Κυδαθηναιεὺς ἐ
[γραμμά]τευεν, 'Αρίστυλλος 'Ερχι[ε]
[ὺς ἐπεσ]τάτει· *vacat*
vacat 0.215
[ἔδο]ξεν τῆι βουλῆι καὶ τῶι δήμωι· *vacat* non-stoichedon
[Διό]φ[αντος ε]ἶπεν·

where a similar 'pseudo-superscript' in old style is followed by the enactment formula in a line by itself.

Cf. also ii^{2}128 (Tod 159), 365/5:

['Επ'] 'Ελπίνο ἄρ[χοντος]· non-stoichedon
anaglyphum
[Ν]εοπολιτ[ῶν]
[Δη]μοσθένους τοῦ Θεοξ[ένου]
[Δι]ο[σκ]ουρίδου τοῦ 'Αμειψ[ίου].
stoichedon 47
['Επὶ] τῆς ['Αντι]ο[χ]ίδος ἐνάτης πρυτανείας ἧι Λυσ[ίας Λυσ ....]
[..]Π̣ι̣θεύ[ς] ἐγρα[μ]μάτευεν· τῶν προέδρων ἐπεψήφ[ιζε Καλλιστ]
[ογε]ίτων [Φ]η[γ]α[εύ]ς· *vacat*
[ἔδο]ξεν [τῆι] βουλῆι καὶ τῶι δήμωι· Πολύευκτο[ς εἶπεν·

[35] The epistates formula is postponed here: cf. ii^{2}43 (Tod 123), 378/7, where it also appears between the enactment formula and the orator.

where a genuine superscript (vv. 1-4) is followed by a new style prescript which is interrupted in v. 8 to allow the enactment formula to occupy a position at the beginning of a line.[36]

All four examples just quoted reflect both the old and the new: the enactment formula is so positioned as to disguise the fact that it is no longer functioning as the introductory item in an old style prescript.

Yet another document further illustrates the unwillingness of secretaries completely to break with the old: ii²106 (Tod 135), 368/7:

'Επὶ Ναυσιγένος ἄρχοντος ἐπὶ τῆς Αἰα[ντίδος ἑ] stoichedon
βδόμης πρυτανείας, Μόσχος Θεστίο Κυδ[αθηναεὺς]
ἐγραμμ[άτε]υε· ἔδοξεν τε͂ι βολε͂ι καὶ τῶ[ι δήμωι· Αἰ]
αντὶς [ἐπ]ρυτάνευε, Παράμυθος 'Οτρυν[εὺς ἐπεστά]
τει, Μόσχος Θεστίο Κυδαθηνα[εὺ]ς ἐγ[ραμμάτευεν,]
Διόφαντος εἶπεν·

This opens as if totally in the new style,[37] but in v. 3 the elegant flow comes to a sudden halt before the intrusion of the enactment formula, followed by the four main items of the old style prescript.[38] It is almost as if the drafter has been unable to free himself from the old compulsion. Cf. also the very fragmentary ii²108, 366/5, a hybrid apparently of the same pattern.

A further 'mixture' is found in ii²206, 349/8:[39]

Θεο[ί].
'Επὶ τῆς Πανδιονίδος ἐνάτης π[ρυτα] stoichedon 28
νείας ἧι Διεύχης Δημάρχου Φρε[άρρ]
ιος ἐγραμμάτευεν· Σωκέρδης 'Αλ[αιε]
ὺς ἐπεστάτει, Καλλίμαχος ἦρχεν· [ἔδ]
οξεν τῆι βουλῆι καὶ τῶι δήμωι· 'Ιε[ρο]
κλείδης Τιμοστράτου 'Αλωπεκῆθε[ν]
εἶπεν·

Here we could well have expected the archon to begin the proceedings in his new form, ἐπὶ Καλλιμάχου ἄρχοντος, but no: in old style formulation he appears in old style position (immediately

[36] Cf. also ii²99, 375/4.
[37] The omission of ἧι with the secretary formula is quite common.
[38] Note the appearance of the epistates before the secretary.
[39] See Pečírka p. 46. θεο[ί] is cut in larger letters right under the cornice.

after the epistates), whereas the enactment formula finds itself in its new style position, just before the orator.

These then are some examples of the variety of formulations current in the first half of the fourth century. The impression one gains from a study of this period is one of considerable concern with the formal aspects of drafting decrees but, as yet, no hard and fast pattern predominates.[40] About the nearest we come to the later stereotyped pattern is perhaps ii^{2}130, 355/4, which I quote in full as a basis for future comparison: [41]

[Π]ροξενία Σ[ω]χάρει Χάρητος Ἀπο[λλωνιάτηι].
[ἐπὶ Καλλι]στράτου ἄρχοντος ἐπὶ τ[ῆ] stoichedon 28
[ς Πανδιο]νίδος πέμπτης πρυτανεί[α]
[ς ἧι Πάνδ]ιος Σωκλέος ἐξ Οἴο ἐγρα[μ]
[μάτευεν]· τρίτηι τῆς πρυτανείας· τ[ῶ]
[ν προέδρ]ων ἐπεψήφι[ζ]εν Γλαυκέτη[ς]
. . . .^{8}. . . .ν· ἔδοξεν τῆι βουλῆι καὶ [τ]
[ῶι δήμωι· Ἀ]ριστοφῶ[ν] εἶπεν·

E. *Patronymics and demotics*

I do not propose to cite exhaustive statistics for the frequency with which patronymics and/or demotics appear or do not appear with the names of secretaries and epistatai, but a few comments must certainly be made.

(1) Secretaries: The tendency is very much for secretaries in prescripts to have both the patronymic and demotic.[42] I have noted only three instances of secretaries with neither, all in old style and all with superscripts in which the secretary appears with paternal and demotic assignation.[43]

In only one instance is the secretary completely omitted: ii^{2}77 II, *ante* 378/7. However, the explanation of the curtailed form of this prescript in general is almost certainly to be found in the fact that this is the decree mentioned in vv. 7-8 on the same stone,

[40] It is instructive to compare different decrees drafted in different ways by the same secretary: e.g. ii^{2}134, 135, 136, 137, all from the year 354/3; and ii^2 206, 207, 208, 209, all of 349/8.

[41] For v. 1 see *S.* xix 49.

[42] First appearance in old style prescript, ii^{2}16 (Tod 103), 394/3; in new style, ii^{2}18 (Tod 108), 394/3. From the late 360s secretaries normally have both tags.

[43] ii^{2}28 (Tod 114), 387/6; ii^{2}77 I, *ante* 378/7; ii^{2}44 (Tod 124), 378/7.

here presented in abbreviated form. It has not been deemed necessary in the circumstances to name the secretary of the earlier decree.[44]

(2) Epistatai: Apart from four examples, all in old style prescripts,[45] all epistatai show the demotic,[46] whether or not the old or new formula is employed for this item. In three instances the epistates does not appear at all.[47]

In dealing with patronymics and demotics it is appropriate to include reference to the orator, for at this period he too begins to share this tendency for greater precision of detail. As from 354/3 orators customarily bear both patronymic and demotic:[48] indeed the evidence suggests that an official decision must lie behind the invariable attachment of these tags once the practice is first attested.[49]

F. *Truncated prescripts*

Three prescripts appear in a much reduced form:

(1) ii^{2}107 (Tod 131), vv. 35-7, honours for Mytilene, 369/8:

[ἐπὶ Λυ]σιστράτου ἄρχοντος· ἔδοξεν τῆ[ι] stoichedon 31
[βουλῆι] καὶ τῶι δήμωι· Καλλίστρατος [εἶ]
[πεν·

The first decree inscribed on this stone was passed in the seventh prytany of the year 368/7. Below it is inscribed this decree, referred to in vv. 20-22, passed in 369/8 in response to Hieroitas and his embassy from Mytilene. No doubt the abbreviated form of the prescript of this second decree is to be explained by the circumstances of its publication: all that it was felt necessary to indicate was the year (the archon), the formula of legal enactment and the orator.

---

[44] See section F below. In the decree in question clearly the earlier decree had not actually been inscribed.

[45] ii^{2}26, between 394 and 387; ii^{2}28 (Tod 114), 387/6; ii^{2}58, *ante* 378/7; ii^{2}110 (Tod 143), 363/2.

[46] But not the patronymic. (There is no surely attested example at any period of name-patronymic-demotic ἐπεστάτει [*pace* W. K. Pritchett, *CSCA* v 1972, 164-9, who attempts to restore EM 13230 in this way.])

[47] ii^{2}18 (Tod 108), 394/3; ii^{2}77 II, *ante* 378/7; ii^{2}96 (Tod 126), 375/4.

[48] E.g. ii^{2}136, 354/3; ii^{2}205, 351/0, ii^{2}206, 207, 208 and 209, all 349/8 etc.

[49] Unlike the epistates, there is no example of an orator with demotic alone.

We might compare ii²77 II, vv. 9-10, *ante* 378/7. The first decree on this stone is a resolution of the boule [50] to publish a proxeny decree for Komaios previously resolved by the ecclesia: it so resolves with the enactment formula ἔδοξεν τῆι βουλῆι κατὰ τὸ τοῦ δήμου ψήφισμα. Decree II presents only the same enactment formula,[51] the tribe in prytany and the orator. Presumably the omission of the archon indicates that both resolutions belong to the same year.[52] The only details therefore considered necessary were the enactment formula (perhaps properly ἔδοξεν τῶι δήμωι), the tribe in prytany and the orator.

(2) *S.* xvii 19, a commercial agreement of some sort between Athens and Siphnos, *c.* 362-355, is quite different:

Θ ε [ο ί]. stoichedon 26
Ἐνάτης πρυτανεί[ας, ἕκτηι καὶ τρ]-
ιακοστῆι· ἔδ[οξεν τῆι βολῆι καὶ τ]-
ῶι δήμ[ω]ι·

Here we have not merely an attenuated prescript but one of most unusual form. The name of the archon and secretary, and possibly also of the prytanising tribe, may well have appeared somewhere above the relief sculpture which is evident above the introductory θε[οί].[53] Even so, the way in which the prytany ordinal and the day of the prytany have been combined is unparalleled. And there seems to be no mention of epistates or orator.[54]

(3) ii²125 (Tod 154), Athens and Eretria, 357/6: the prescript consists solely of

[ἔδοξεν τῶι δ]ήμωι· Ἡγήσ[ι]ππ[ος εἶπεν· stoichedon 39

the enactment formula and the orator. However, since Tod describes this stone as "complete only on the left," perhaps one can simply assume that the beginning of this text is missing.

---

[50] See above p. 16.
[51] Probably wrongly repeated from v. 2.
[52] The orator too may be identical.
[53] See Woodhead *H.* xxvi 231-3, 87. Woodhead compares ii²164, where these details appear to have been given on the pediment and architrave surmounting the stele.
[54] Woodhead adduces ii²14 and 97 (not 27), texts of alliances which lack the usual prescript, only to reject their evidence as parallels here. No real explanation of this text has in fact yet been offered.

CHAPTER THREE

THE YEARS 349 TO 321 [1]

A. *Superscripts*

In the last chapter we considered the growing prominence of the archon at the expense of the secretary as reflected in superscripts. By the middle of the fourth century neither official commonly appeared superscript: the last example of a secretary in such a position is ii^{2}127 (Tod 157), 356/5;[2] the archon appears in ii^{2}116 (Tod 147), 361/0; ii^{2}128 (Tod 159) and ii^{2}129, both 356/5, and only again,[3] it seems, in ii^{2}406, dated *c.* 332 in the *Corpus*.[4]

Although, therefore, secretaries do not now appear superscript at all, one interesting and unusual prescript, ii^{2}348, 331/0, has been laid out in such a way as to give considerable prominence to the name of the secretary: [5]

['Επὶ 'Αριστοφάνους] non-stoichedon
[ἄρχοντος ἐπὶ τῆς 'Ακα]
μα[ντίδος ὀγδόης· ἐνάτηι]
ἐπὶ δέ[κα, ἕκτηι τῆς πρυτανείας·]
ἐκκλησί[α ἐν Διονύσου· τῶν προέδρων]
ἐπεψήφιζ[εν . . . . 22 . . . .]
vacat 0.015
Νικόστρατος 'Α̣[ρχελέω ἐκ Μυρρινούττης ἐγραμμάτευεν].
vacat 0.045
Φιλέας 'Αν[τιγένου Παιονίδης εἶπεν·] stoichedon 29

All in all this is an unusual text: [6] whether due to the instruction

---

[1] Some 55 prescripts form the basis of study for this chapter.

[2] Discussed above p. 21.

[3] In ii^{2}349 (Tod 193), 331/0, the archon formula ἐπὶ 'Αριστοφάνους ἄρχοντος is cut in larger letters in a line of its own, giving it the appearance of being part of the preceding superscript. In fact, however, it is the first line of the prescript.

[4] For the possibility that this stone joins with ii^{2}129, see above p. 23 note 13.

[5] For the secretary's patronymic and demotic see *TAY* p. 90.

[6] For the omission of πρυτανείας (v. 3) see p. 26 above; and of the enactment formula, see pp. 44-45 below. For the appearance of the epistates before the secretary see p. 5 above and p. 36 below.

of the drafter or to the artistry of the cutter [7] we cannot be sure, although we may tend to favour the former view.

Not only do archon and secretary disappear from superscripts but superscripts of any kind—with the exception of the ubiquitous θεοί— [8] become less and less common as time goes on. They tend to be confined to a few headings giving the names of the honorands in the nominative,[9] genitive,[10] or dative.[11] The only other formulation of any frequency is προξενία (*vel sim.*) + dative of the recipient:[12] examples of this type restored with the genitive are probably erroneous and should be corrected to the dative.[13]

B. *Prescripts in general*

Very few traces of old style now remain. ii^{2}227, perhaps of 342/1, exhibits the mixture of old and new which we commented on above: [14]

[᾿Επὶ Σωσιγένου]ς ἄρ[χοντος] stoichedon 21
[ἐπὶ τῆς Αἰγηΐ]δος ὀγδ[όης π]
[ρυτανείας· ἔ]δοξεν τῆι βου
[λῆι καὶ τῶ]ι δήμωι· Αἰγηΐς ἐ
[πρυτάνευε], Καλλιάδης Εὐω
[νυμεὺς ἐγραμμά]τευε, Τιμ.
[- - - ἐπεστάτει? - - - - -]

Although the prescript is in an extremely fragmentary condition, enough is preserved to allow us to be sure that it begins with two items in new style (archon and prytanising tribe), then reverts to an old style formulation introduced by the enactment formula.[15]

[7] The shape of the prescript is reminiscent of the Hellenistic 'trick poems.'

[8] Note the unique superscript to ii^{2}218, 346/5:

θεοὶ Ἄβδηρος Ἀθηνάα. Διοσκουρίδης
Διονυσοδώρου.

where θεοί is defined by naming the eponymous deity of Abdera and Athena alongside the chief recipient of the honours decreed.

[9] E.g. ii^{2}349 (Tod 193), 331/0.

[10] E.g. ii^{2}238, 338/7; ii^{2}351 + 624 (Tod 198), 330/29.

[11] ii^{2}212 (Tod 167), 347/6.

[12] E.g. ii^{2}231, 340/39; ii^{2}357, 327/6; cf. earlier ii^{2}129, 356/5; ii^{2}130 (see *S.* xix 49), 355/4; ii^{2}133, 355/4 etc.

[13] So ii^{2}416, *c.* 330; ii^{2}419, *post* 336/5.

[14] P. 30.

[15] Cf. ii^{2}213 (Tod 168), 347/6, which opens with ἐπὶ Θεμιστοκλέους ἄρχοντος but then continues with the enactment formula followed by a list of items in old style.

ii²233 (Tod 175), 340/39, is, if correctly restored, a curious mixture of old and new:

stoichedon 37

[᾿Ε]πὶ Θε[οφράστου ἄρχο]ντο[ς· ἔδοξεν τῶι δήμωι· Κε]
κροπὶ[ς ἐπρυτάνευε]ν, ὀγδό[ηι τῆς πρυτανείας· τ]
ῶν προέ[δρων ἐπ]εψήφισεν [16] Σ . . . . .¹⁶. . . . . . .
. . · ἐγραμμάτευεν Ἄσπετος [Δημοστράτου Κυθήρ]·
[Κα]λλικράτης Χαροπίδου [Λαμπτρεὺς εἶπεν·

Opening with the new style ἐπὶ Θεοφράστου ἄρχοντος, it then continues with the enactment formula and Κεκροπὶς ἐπρυτάνευεν, suggesting that the text will now proceed as, e.g., in ii²227 and 213 (Tod 168). Instead, however, we come next to the day of the prytany, the epistates in new style (and preceding the secretary),[17] and the secretary item in a most unusual order, with the verb before the name of the official.[18] This last aberration may be accounted for thus: having just completed cutting the name of the epistates—which, of course, in the new formulation *follows* its verb—the cutter confusedly thought that he had just inscribed the name of the secretary, and so he continued with ἐγραμμάτευεν. He then 'remedied' the situation by cutting the secretary's name next after the verb.[19]

ii²349 (Tod 193), 331/0, is a further instance of the phenomenon I commented on above:[20]

῾Ρηβούλας Σεύθου: ὑὸς Κότυος ἀδελφὸς ᾿Ανγελ[ῆθεν].
Θ ε ο [ί].
᾿Επὶ ᾿Αριστοφάνους ἄρχοντος
ἐπὶ τῆς Κε[κ]ροπίδος δεκάτης πρυτα — stoichedon 28
νείας· Σκ[ιρ]οφοριῶνος δεκάτηι ἱσ[τ]
αμένου, [ἕκτ]ει καὶ δεκάτει τῆς πρυ[τ]
ανεία[ς· τῶν] προέδρων ἐπεψή[φι]ζε [Δω]
ρόθε[ος ῾Αλ]αιεύς· *vacat*

---

[16] For the tense ἐπεψήφισεν cf. ii²354, 328/7; ii²361, 325/4. No significance should be read into the use of the aorist in these instances.

[17] Cf. ii²225, 343/2; ii²228 (Tod 174), 341/0; ii²348, 331/0 during this period.

[18] The same order is found in ii²339a (see *TAY* p. 48), 333/2: ἧι ἐγρ[αμμάτευεν ᾿Αρχέ]|[λας Χα]ιρίου Πα[λληνεύς.

[19] The prescript as a whole is so confused that it is hard to decide where confusion ends and deliberate choice begins.

[20] Pp. 28-30.

non-stoichedon

ἔδοξεν [τῆι βουλ]ῆι καὶ τῶι δήμωι· Νόθ[ιππος Λυσίου Διο]
μειεύ[ς εἶπε·

Here the enactment formula is isolated at the beginning of a fresh line, thus apparently in initial position as in old style.

These few examples are enough to show that the old had not yet completely succumbed to the new, but the end was not far. The new style prescript, with its greater complexity and sophistication of syntax and form, is now fully and firmly established.

C. *Month and day of month*

In the last chapter we saw how greater detail of date was achieved by adding the ordinal numeral to the name of the prytanising tribe and by specifying the day of the prytany. Now for the first time we find mention of the lunar month and/or the day within the month. The conjunction of this item with the day of the prytany furnishes a so-called 'calendar equation', in which the date by the festival calendar can be squared with the date by the conciliar calendar.

The first movement in this direction is seen in ii^{2}229 (*c.* Add. p. 659), 341/0,[21] where the day is given in terms of both calendars:

[Θ ε]ο[ί].

stoichedon 38

['Επὶ Νικομάχου ἄρχοντος ἐπ]ὶ τῆς Λεων[τίδ]ο[ς δεκ]
[άτης πρυτανείας ἧι 'Ονήσι]ππος Σμικύ[θο] 'Α[ραφήν]
[ιος ἐγραμμάτευεν· ἕνηι κα]ὶ [ν]έαι ἑβδ[όμηι] κ[αὶ τρ]
[ιακοστῆι τῆς πρυτανεία]ς· κτλ.

Here, although the lunar day is given (ἕνη καὶ νέα), the name of the month (almost certainly Skirophorion) [22] is omitted. Omission of the name of the month is, in fact, not uncommon, and seems particularly characteristic in the case of the last day of the month,[23] although it also occurs with other days.[24]

---

[21] See *TAY* p. 10.

[22] On Meritt's analysis the equation would be ‹Skirophorion› 30 = Prytany [X] [37] = 383rd day of the year.

[23] So ii^{2}330 III (*TAY* p. 79), 336/5; ii^{2}330 I (*TAY* p. 79), 335/4; ii^{2}331 (*TAY* p. 81), 335/4; ii^{2}354 (*TAY* pp. 96-7: ἕνη καὶ νέα προτέρα), 328/7; ii^{2}357 (*TAY* p. 98), 327/6.

[24] ii^{2}330 II (*TAY* p. 78), 336/5; ii^{2}348 (*TAY* pp. 90-1), 331/0; ii^{2}356 (Tod 199; *TAY* pp. 98-9), 327/6; ii^{2}360 (*TAY* p. 102), 325/4.

The earliest example in which both the name and the day of the month are given appears to be ii^{2}237 (*c.* Add. p. 659) (Tod 178), 338/7:

stoichedon 41

[᾿Επὶ Χαιρών]δου ἄρχο[ντος ἐπὶ τῆς Πανδιονίδος δ]ε[κ]ά
[της] π[ρυτα]νείας ἧι Φ[ίλιππος ᾿Αντιφήμου Εἰρεσίδης]
[ἐγρ]αμ[μά]τευεν· Θαργη[λιῶνος δευτέραι φθίνοντος, ἕ]
[κτη]ι [τῆ]ς πρυτανείας· κτλ.[25]

Slightly earlier we have the first example of the type in which the month only (in the genitive) is given, with no indication of the number of the day: *S.* xvi 52, 339/8, has been restored to read:

stoichedon 39

[᾿Επ]ὶ τῆς Πα̣[νδ]ι̣ον̣ί̣δος δ̣[εκ]ά̣τ̣ης [πρυτανείας ἧι Φαῖδρος]
[Με]ί̣δ̣ωνος Χ[ο]λ̣λ[ε]ί(δης) ἐγραμμά[τευεν· Σκιροφοριῶνος(?)·] [26]
[δε]υ̣τέραι καὶ τριακοστῆι τῆς πρυ[τανείας· τῶν προέδρ]
[ων ἐπεψ]ή̣φιζεν Καλλί̣α̣ς Φρεάρ[ρι]ος· ἔ[δοξεν τῶι δήμωι·]
[Τηλ]έ̣μαχος Θ[εα]γγέλου ᾿Αχαρνεὺς ε[ἶπεν·

Once this feature has appeared, it is found regularly in prescripts, usually in the form with both elements, day of month and day of prytany.[27] In four instances, however, neither item is included,[28] and in two cases the day of the month is found without the day of the prytany.[29] In one example (after 341/0) the day of the prytany appears alone: [30] but since there is reason to believe that this text is only a summary of a full prescript set up privately, we may ignore the phenomenon as far as official practice goes.

D. *Indication of the type of meeting and its venue*

Another innovation of this period is the inclusion of ἐκκλησία in the prescript, first instanced in ii^{2}330 III, 336/5:

---

[25] See *TAY* pp. 74-6 for a discussion of the possible restorations.

[26] Cf. ii^{2}365 (*TAY* p. 106), 323/2: ῾Εκατομβαιῶν]|[ο]ς· ἑνδεκάτει τῆς πρυτανεί[ας where either haplography or lack of need may explain the omission of the lunar day. Hekatombaion 11 = Prytany I 11 = 11th day of the year.

[27] E.g. ii^{2}242 (*TAY* p. 77), 337/6; *S.* xxi 272 (*TAY* p. 80), 335/4; ii^{2}336a (*TAY* p. 82), 334/3 etc.

[28] ii^{2}240 (Tod 181) and ii^{2}241, same day 337/6; ii^{2}243, also 337/6 (which suggests that the secretary of this year was not particularly impressed with the new idea, although he had himself tried it out in the sixth prytany, ii^{2}239 (*TAY* p. 76)); ii^{2}337 (Tod 189), 333/2.

[29] ii^{2}335 (*S.* xxi 274), 334/3 and ii^{2}454 (*S.* xxi 293), 324/3.

[30] ii^{2}366 (*TAY* pp. 106-7), 323/2.

stoichedon 58

['Επ]ὶ Πυθοδήλου ἄρχοντος ἐπ[ὶ τῆς . . .6. . . ἴδος δεκάτης πρυτα]
[ν]είας· ἕνει καὶ νέαι, ἑβδόμη[ι καὶ τριακοστῆι τῆς πρυτανεία]
[ς]· ἐκκλησία· τῶν προέδρων ἐπε[ψήφιζε . . . . .19. . . . .]
ἔδοξεν τῆι βουλῆι καὶ τῶι δ[ήμωι· Ἱπποχάρης. . . .9. . . . 'Αλωπ]
εκῆθεν εἶπεν·

This proves to be the normal position for the item, immediately after the day of the prytany. Cf. also ii^{2}330 I, 335/4.

The first occurrence of ἐκκλησία κυρία is of approximately the same period, ii^{2}336a, 334/3. Mention of the venue,[31] ἐκκλησία ἐν Διονύσου, has been restored first in ii^{2}345, 332/1 and is clearly to be read in ii^{2}350, now again placed in 318/7.[32] Note also ἐκκλησία κυρία ἐν τῶι θεάτρωι, first in ii^{2}389 (*S.* xxi 354), 293/2.

As for meetings of the Council, βουλή, unlike ἐκκλησία, is never found without qualification: the place of meeting is always included. βουλὴ ἐμ βουλευτηρίωι appears first in the bouleutic resolution in ii^{2}330 II, 336/5, again immediately after the day of the prytany. Clearly the secretary of the year 335/4 [33] was concerned with (? the decision to include) specification of the type of meeting, although there is no such specification in a prescript of the fourth prytany of 336/5.[34]

E. *Mention of* συμπρόεδροι, *with or without lists of their names* [35]

From perhaps 378/7 [36] the presidency of the boule (and also of the ecclesia if it had a meeting on that day) was held by a one-day committee known as the proedroi, chosen by lot by the epistates of the prytaneis one each from all the tribes except the one in prytany.[37] Thus in the period of the ten tribes the committee consisted of nine men, the Chairman (ἐπιστάτης τῶν προέδρων) and eight colleagues; in the period of the twelve tribes, it was a committee of eleven, the Chairman and ten colleagues.

---

[31] For the various meeting-places of the ecclesia and boule see W. A. McDonald, *The Political Meeting Places of the Greeks*, (Johns Hopkins Studies in Archaeology, xxxiv), Baltimore, 1943.

[32] See Meritt, *H.* xlv 1976, 173.

[33] The date of publication of ii^{2}330 as a whole.

[34] ii^{2}328.

[35] On this entire subject see S. Dow, "The Preambles of Athenian Decrees Containing Lists of Symproedroi," *H.* xxxii 1963, 335-365.

[36] See Lewis, *BSA* xlix 1954, 31-4; Rhodes, *op. cit.*, 26-7.

[37] See Arist. *Ath. Pol.* 44.1-3.

From *c.* 341 the new style of formula, τῶν προέδρων ἐπεψήφιζεν ὁ δεῖνα, becomes the standard form [38]; and from 333/2 the symproedroi are also mentioned,[39] at first paratactically, the word συμπρόεδροι appearing (without καί) after the name of the chairman, followed by a list of their names and demotics. The first preserved decree listing symproedroi is ii^{2}336 III (*c.* Add. p. 659), now certainly dated in 333/2: [40]

['Ελαφ]ηβολιῶνος ἕνε[ι καὶ νέαι, ἕκτει κα] stoichedon 31
[ὶ εἰκ]οστεῖ τῆς πρυτ[ανείας ἧι 'Αρχέλας]
[Παλλ]ηνεὺς ἐγραμμά[τευεν· ἐκκλησία· τῶ]
[ν προ]έδρων ἐπεψήφι[ζεν . . . . . 12 . . . . .]
. . 5 . .ς· συμπρόεδρο[ι· . . . . . . 14 . . . . . .]
. . 5 . ., Θυμοχάρης Ṭε[ιθράσιος, . . . ? . . .]
[Κυδαθ]ηναιεύς, Εὔξεν[. . . . . . 14 . . . . . .]
. . 5 . .ος Κεφαλῆθεν, Ẹ[. . . . . . 14 . . . . . .]
[. . . 'Ελ]ευσίνιος, Νικι[. . . . . . 14 . . . . . .]
. . 5 . .ης 'Αριστάρχου Φ̣[. . . . . . . εἶπεν·

The phenomenon occurs in several other decrees of this period,[41] all of which (with one exception) can be restored to yield a text τῶν προέδρων ἐπεψήφιζεν ὁ δεῖνα· συμπρόεδροι· LIST. The 'exception' is ii^{2}545, ?321/0,[42] where we read:

---

[38] The last example of ὁ δεῖνα ἐπεστάτει seems to be ii^{2}225, 343/2 (possibly ii^{2}227, 342/1, although the stone breaks off at the crucial point.)

[39] The question why the symproedroi came to be listed has never really been discussed. Dow (*art. cit.*, p. 339) remarks that the listing gave added impressiveness to the prescript and "might conceivably be due to mere assiduity on the part of the Secretary, or to vanity on the part of the Symproedroi." It is clear, of course, why the board existed: "to some extent they shared the legal responsibility." But, whatever the explanation of the listing of their names, we should note that the lists are very sporadic—only in some 22 prescripts between 333/2 and the 220s. On the other hand, the addition of καὶ συμπρόεδροι (without list) to the chairman formula is the norm from *c.* 320 (ii^{2}374, which can now be dated close to ii^{2}373, as one would wish) to the second century A.D.

[40] See Dow, *art. cit.*, pp. 341-2. (For the curtailed form of the prescript see p. 46 below.)

[41] ii^{2}727 (*S.* xxi 324), between *c.* 330 and 308/7 (but see Meritt, *H.* xxxii 1963, 439); ii^{2}452 (*S.* xxi 284), 328/7; ii^{2}800 (*S.* xxi 289), ?326/5; ii^{2}547 (*S.* xxi 292), 324/3; ii^{2}454 (*S.* xxi 293), 324/3; ii^{2}546 (*S.* xxi 304), 321/0. ii^{2}378 (*S.* xxi 353) is probably to be dated 294/3, thus spoiling Dow's neat dividing line of 307/6 for the appearance of the patronymic of the chairman (see Meritt, *H.* xxxii 1963, 429-31 and 439).

[42] See *S.* xxiv 106.

τῶν προ]
[έδρων ἐπεψήφιζεν. . . . Κόπ]ρειος καὶ οἱ συμπρόεδ
[ροι· . . . . .^{10}. . . . 'Αριστοκρά?]τους Πόριος εἶπεν·

The appearance of οἱ is almost without parallel,[43] and perhaps (at this period) best treated as a slip. More important is the observation that this seems to be the earliest example (if correctly dated) of mention of the symproedroi without a list of their names.[44] From this time on καὶ συμπρόεδροι (without list) is the regular formulation of this item in the prescript.

It should be noted carefully that Dow's remark "Down to a year which may be specified as 307/6, when doubtless many changes were made, the Chairman's patronymic is never given; after that year, always" [45] applies only to documents in which actual lists of names of symproedroi are given.[46] The first example of a chairman with patronymic is in a text which has καὶ συμπρόεδροι *but no list*: ii^{2}450, 314/13:

τῶν προέδρων ἐπεψήφι — stoichedon 21
ζεν 'Αριστοκράτης 'Αριστο
δήμου Οἰν καὶ συμπρόεδρο
ι· Θρασυκλῆς Ναυσικράτο[υ]
ς Θριάσι εἶπεν·

This, in fact, is the only certain example of a chairman with patronymic, even in texts without lists, before the creation of the Macedonian tribes.[47] However, the patronymic may possibly be restored in several texts of the intervening years, especially if allowance is made for abbreviated demotics.[48]

F. *Patronymics and demotics*

I turn now to a related phenomenon, the omission of patronymic and/or demotic in cases where we have come to expect their presence:

[43] Only at ii^{2}1077, A.D. 209/10, and restored in *S*. xxi 504, *paullo post* A.D. 196.
[44] ii^{2}374 is another early example, and should be dated *c*. 320 to tie in with ii^{2}373.
[45] *Art. cit.*, p. 340.
[46] And even in those cases there is some reason to query the exquisiteness of Dow's table: see Meritt, *art. cit.*, p. 439.
[47] The next indisputable example is ii^{2}358 (*S*. xxi 326), 307/6 (as restored), or ii^{2}471, 306/5.
[48] E.g. *S*. xxi 316, 319/18; ii^{2}453, 310/09.

(1) Secretary without demotic: The customary formula at this time is, of course, ἧι name-patronymic-demotic ἐγραμμάτευεν. In ii²365, 323/2 we read: [49]

πρυτα[νείας ἧι Ἀρχίας] stoichedon 32
[Π]υθοδώρου ἐγραμμάτευε[ν·

Contrast ii²367,[50] of the same year:

ἧι Ἀρχίας Πυθ]οδώρου Ἀλωπεκ stoichedon 26
[ῆθεν ἐγραμμάτευ]εν·

Since the phenomenon is unparalleled, one must assume that the explanation is a mere slip on the part of the drafter or cutter.[51]

(2) Secretary without patronymic: [52] In ii²228 (Tod 174), 341/0 the secretary appears after the chairman [53] in the following form:

τῶν προέδρων ἐπεψήφιζ[ε] stoichedon 26
ν Ἀριστόμαχος ἐξ Οἴου, Ὀνήσιππο
ς Ἀραφήνιος ἐγραμμάτευεν.

Contrast ii²229 (*c.* Add. p. 659), of the same year:

πρυτανείας ἧι Ὀνήσι]ππος Σμικύ[θο] Ἀ[ραφήν] stoichedon 38
[ιος ἐγραμμάτευεν·

Cf. also ii²242, 337/6:

πρυτανείας· Χαιρέστρατος Ἀ] stoichedon 33
χαρνεὺς ἐγ[ραμμάτευεν· [54]

and ii²336 III, 333/2 [55]:

---

[49] See *TAY* p. 106. The secretary's name is wrongly given in the *Corpus* (see *S.* xxi 294).
[50] *TAY* p. 107.
[51] The omission of ἑνδεκάτει with the lunar month in the same document *may*, as we have seen above, p. 38 note 26, be put down to carelessness: but not necessarily so.
[52] Cf. ii²99, 375/4: see above p. 31.
[53] Cf. ii²225, 343/2; ii²233 (Tod 175), 340/39; ii²348, 331/0.
[54] It is not possible to accommodate the patronymic by the expedient of omitting the preceding πρυτανείας from the lacuna: for Ἀμεινίου occupies only 8 letter spaces (for the patronymic see e.g. ii²240 (Tod 181)).
[55] For the date and form of this document as a whole see Dow, *H.* xxxii 1963, 341-2, and Meritt, *ibid.* 434-5. See also below p. 46.

πρυτ[ανείας ἧι 'Αρχέλας] stoichedon 31
[Παλλ]ηνεὺς ἐγραμμά[τευεν·

Perhaps then in the case of the omission of the patronymic we have a recognised formulation, not just mere error.

(3) Orator with nomen alone: We have come to expect the orator to appear without exception in the form name-patronymic-demotic. It is surprising, therefore, to read in ii^{2}366, 323/2:

'Επὶ Κηφισοδώρου non-stoichedon
ἄρχοντος ἐπὶ τῆς Αἰγ
ηΐδος δευτέρας πρυτα
νείας· ἕκτηι καὶ δεκά
τηι τῆς πρυτανείας·
τῶν προέδρων
ἐπεψήφιζεν 'Ηγ
ησίας Μαραθώνιος·
[ἔδο]ξεν τῶι δή[μ]ωι· 'Αρι
. . .^{6}. . . εἶπεν·

where there is presumably no room to accomodate any more than the missing letters of the nomen. Here the explanation is neither deliberate choice nor mere slip: as Wilhelm saw, this text is a mere summary of a full text and was probably set up at private expense.[56]

G. *Omitted items*

Other substantial omissions also occur in prescripts at this time:

(1) Omission of secretary: In the prescript quoted in full above it is noticeable that the secretary is not included. Similar omission of this official occurs in other texts where again the explanation may be either that the text in question was to be published privately or not at all. E.g. ii^{2}330 II and III, both 336/5, texts in honour of Phyleus the hieropoios, were presumably not originally intended for publication; [57] ii^{2}337 (Tod 189), 333/2, giving permission to the merchants of Kitium to found a sanctuary of Aphrodite in Attica, was probably inscribed at the expense of the Kitians themselves;

[56] In the decree proper no provision is made for publishing the document.
[57] ii^{2}330 I, 335/4, makes provision for their publication.

ii^{2}349 (Tod 193), 331/0, honouring Rheboulas the Odrysian, may also have been set up by the honorand himself.[58]

(2) Omission of the epistates: The chairman does not appear in ii^{2}215, 346/5, but why this should be so is not clear.

(3) Omission of orator: ii^{2}356 (*c.* Add. p. 660) (Tod 199), 327/6, appears to be lacking the orator: for it seems impossible to fit the item in after the enactment formula, using the letters which have been restored in the *Corpus* as:

. . . ? . . . ἔδοξ[ε]ν [τῶι] δήμω stoichedon 20
[ι· . . . . .]ημ[.]μνω[.]τ. .α. .

No name . . . . .]ημ[έ]μνω[ν] seems instanced.

Another example of omission may occur in ii^{2}225, 343/2, a somewhat unusual prescript to an alliance with the Messenians:[59]

['Επὶ Πυθοδότου ἄρχοντος ἐ]πὶ τῆς Αἰγεῖδος non-stoichedon
[δεκάτης πρυτανείας· τετά]ρτηι τῆς πρυτανείας·
[ἔδοξεν τῶι δήμωι· 'Αρχικ]λείδης Παιανιεὺς
[ἐπεστάτει· Κλεόστρατος Τιμο]σθένους Αἰγιλιεὺς ἐ
[γραμμάτευεν]· *vacat* συμμαχία τοῦ [δήμ]
[ου τοῦ 'Αθηναίων καὶ - - ων καὶ] Μεσσηνίω[ν καὶ]
- -

But the form of this prescript warns against drawing any firm conclusions. After the *vacat* συμμαχία κτλ. reads suspiciously like a *title*[60] (rather than the beginning of the terms of the alliance), and it may well be that the orator appeared after this title, immediately before the terms proper began.

(4) Omission of the enactment formula: such omission is not at all uncommon, as indeed is also the case in decrees of the late third

[58] In another text, ii^{2}359, 326/5, the secretary appears to have been omitted, but could have come after the epistates. Nothing of the decree proper is preserved.

[59] Note that the epistates precedes the secretary: Archikleides must be the epistates, since we know from ii^{2}224 that Kleostratos was the secretary of this year. For other examples see p. 42 note 53.

[60] Cf. ii^{2}14 (Tod 101), alliance with Boiotia, 395/4; ii^{2}16 (Tod 103), alliance with Eretria, 394/3.

and early second centuries.[61] Examples occur all through this period.[62]

H. *Problems*

(1) ii²224, honours for the Kephallenians, 343/2:

Θ ε [ο ί].
ῆι Κλεόστρατος Τιμοσθένους Αἰ[γιλιεὺς] ἐγραμμάτευεν.
Ἐπὶ Πυθοδότου ἄρχο[ντο]ς ἐπὶ τῆς Αἰγηΐ stoichedon 31
δος δεκάτης· τετάρτ[ηι τ]ῆς πρυτανείας·
τῶν προέδρων ἐπεψή[φι]ζεν Ἀρχικλείδη
ς Παιανιεύς· Ἀρ[ιστοφῶ]ν Ἀριστοφάνους
[Ἀ]ζην[ιε]ὺς εἶπεν·

It is clear what has gone wrong here. The secretary item has been accidentally omitted by the cutter after δεκάτης in v. 4, and presumably the error was not noticed until it was too late to find an alternative spot within the prescript (e.g. after the epistates). Consequently, the item was—somewhat mechanically—[63] inscribed between the superscript θεοί and the first line of the prescript. This is a good illustration of the reluctance to discard a stone because of errors.[64]

(2) *S.* xvi 52, 339/8: This prescript begins with the prytanising tribe, [ἐπ]ὶ τῆς Πα̣[νδ]ι̣ον̣ί̣δος δ̣[εκ]ά̣τ̣ης [πρυτανείας, and then continues with no further anomaly. There is no reason not to suppose that ἐπὶ Λυσιμαχίδου ἄρχοντος was cut somewhere higher on the stone, possible as a quasi-superscript in larger letters.

(3) ii²243, decree in honour of Kalliteles, 337/6: In vv. 5-6 the enactment formula is expressed in a form with the demos *preceding* the boule:

---

[61] See Meritt, *H.* xxix 1960, p. 19.

[62] ii²212 (Tod 167), 347/6; ii²214, 347/6; ii²218, 346/5; ii²224, 343/2; ii²240 (Tod 181), ii²241 and 242, all 337/6; ii²336 III (*c.* Add. p. 659), 333/2; ii²348, 331/0; ii²360 and 361, 325/4.

[63] The situation could have been improved if the mason had had the sense to omit the relative. Indeed, we have no reason to think highly of his workmanship: the omission of πρυτανείας (after δεκάτης) may also be his fault, although the enactment formula possibly did not appear on his draft.

[64] His employer (the State) would also be unlikely to wish to squander a valuable stone.

ἔδοξεν τῶι δ] stoichedon 29
ἥμωι καὶ τεῖ βου[λεῖ·

Clearly this is unintentional and must be put down to the carelessness of the stone-cutter. Presumably he cut ἔδοξεν τῶι δήμωι before he realised that he should have inscribed the full probouleumatic formula: he then repaired the damage by simply tacking on the phrase καὶ τεῖ βουλεῖ. Whether or not this completely unnerved our mason is hard to tell: it certainly did not improve his spelling (Μυριν[ούσιος, v. 7; Καλιτέλης, v. 8; ? ἐκλ]|[ησ]ίαι, vv. 11-12).

(4) ii²336 III, vv. 5 ff., 333/2: [65]

['Ελαφ]ηβολιῶνος ἕνε[ι καὶ νέαι, ἕκτει κα] stoichedon 31
[ὶ εἰκ]οστεῖ τῆς πρυτ[ανείας, ἧι 'Αρχέλας]
[Παλλ]ηνεὺς ἐγραμμά[τευεν· ἐκκλησία· τῶ]
[ν προ]έδρων ἐπεψήφι[ζεν . . . . . 12 . . . . .]
. . 5 . . ς· συμπρόεδρο[ι· κτλ.

It has generally been assumed that the archon was named in decree II,[66] and perhaps also the prytanising tribe.[67] Wherever they appeared, they did not come at the beginning of decree III, thus posing the problem of where and how to accommodate the secretary. The solution employed seems manifestly the neatest in the circumstances: immediately after the word πρυτανείας in the prytany day item. The remainder of the prescript follows without problem.

(5) ii²351 + 624 (Tod 198), 330/29: [68]

[Εὐδήμ]ου Πλαται[έως].
[ἐπὶ 'Αριστ]οφῶντος ἄρχοντο[ς] stoichedon *c.* 24 [69]
[ἐ]π[ὶ τῆς] Λεωντίδος ἐνάτη[ς] π[ρυ]
ταν[εία]ς ἧι 'Αντίδωρος 'Αντί[νου]
Παι[ανι]εὺς ἐγραμμάτευεν: ἐ[ν]
[δ]εκά[τ]ηι Θαργηλιῶνος, ἐνάτη[ι]

[65] For the whole prescript see above p. 40.
[66] As Dow points out (*H.* xxxii 1963, p. 341), this is in fact the main reason for assuming the existence of decree II.
[67] Though we have no way of telling whether the same tribe was in prytany at the time of both decrees or not.
[68] See *TAY* pp. 91-4.
[69] For comment on the stoichedon pattern of this inscription see Pečírka pp. 68-70.

[κ]αὶ δ[ε]κάτηι τῆς πρυτανείας·
[τῶν πρ]οέδρων ἐπεψήφιζεν Ἀγ[τι] [70]
φανη[ς] Εὐωνυμεύς· ἔδοξεν τῶι
[δήμωι]· Λυκοῦργος Λυκόφρονος
[Βουτά]δης εἶπεν·

The anomaly here rests in the lunar date, where we find the extremely rare [71] order ordinal-month, instead of the normal chiastic arrangement of the dates by festival and conciliar calendars. It seems that the drafter (?cutter) may have been in some confusion at this point,[72] for the number of the day of the month appears also to be in error. The equation should read

Thargelion <1> = Prytany IX 19 = 326th day of year.

(6) ii²354, honouring Androkles the priest, 328/7, shows a unique formulation at the beginning of the prescript, where the honorand is included, in a neat chiastic phrase, with the archon: [73]

[Θ ε] ο ί.
[Ἐπ' Εὐθυκρίτου ἄρ]χοντος, ἱερείως δὲ Ἀνδρο stoichedon 34
[κλέους ἐκ Κεραμ]έων·

There is nothing peculiar here, merely a clever variation which enables the honorand to be included in the prescript rather than isolated in the superscript.[74]

(7) *S.* xxi 288, fragment of an honorary decree, 327/6:

[Ἐφ' Ἡγήμονος ἄρχοντ]ος ἐπὶ τῆς Οἰνηΐ[δος ἐ] stoichedon 33
[νάτης πρυτανείας] ἧι Αὐτοκλῆς Αὐτί[ου Ἀχ]
[αρνεὺς ἐγραμμάτε]υεν· Μουνιχιῶνος . . . .
. . . . 16 . . . . . . .ἐνάτει μετ' εἰκά[δας· τ]
[ῶν προέδρων ἐπεψή]φιζεν Πάμφιλος Π[αιαν]

[70] For the name of the chairman see Pečírka p. 69. Antiphanes of Euonymon was epistates in ii²240 and 241, of the same day 337/6.

[71] Cf. ii²546 (*S.* xxi 304), 321/0.

[72] Perhaps the following ἐνάτηι καὶ δεκάτηι produced an erroneous ἐνδεκάτηι in his mind's eye, which he then reproduced on the stone at the wrong point as well.

[73] We will see the same arrangement when we come to deal with the anagrapheis.

[74] The idea does not seem to have caught on. But cf. ii²659 (Sokolowski [1969], 39), 283/2.

[ιεύς· ἔδοξεν τῶι δή]μωι· *vacat*
. . . . .¹⁷. . . . . Θριά[σ]ιος εἶπ[εν·

There are two serious problems here: (i) what letter, if any can be read immediately before ἐνάτει in v. 4; (ii) what is to be restored in the lacuna between the name of the month and the day of the month? These two problems are obviously interrelated.

In the original publication [75] Meritt suggested that the lacuna be filled with ἐκκλησία ἐν τῶι θεάτρωι, a somewhat violent distortion of the natural run of things, which found little favour.[76] Pritchett and Neugebauer [77] read a delta before ἐνάτει and suggested:

Μουνιχιῶνος [δευτ]|[έραι, ἡμερολεγδὸν] δ' ἐνάτει μετ' εἰκά[δας·

which also found little support and was finally dismissed by Meritt, who showed that ἡμερολεγδόν could not be so used.[78] In the meantime Meritt had made another suggestion: [79]

Μουνιχιῶνος· [πέμπ]|[τει τῆς πρυτανεία]ς· ἐνάτει μετ' εἰκά[δας·

again a tortured order which could only be justified by assuming an error in the cutting. Finally Meritt offers: [80]

Μουνιχιῶνος [ἐνάτ]|[ει φθίνοντος, νυνὶ] δ̣' ἐνάτει μετ' εἰκά[δας·

justifying the restoration by the assumption that we have here reflected the change in terminology for the third decade of the month (from φθίνοντος, last recorded 320/19, to μετ' εἰκάδας, first recorded 334/3). But this is still far from certain: no parallel can be drawn from the later double dating κατ' ἄρχοντα and κατὰ θεόν; for, unlike the case in question, there was then some reason to express the day in both forms. We may accept Merritt's suggestion *faute de mieux*, but it is perhaps better to confess that, as yet, we do not really understand what has gone wrong with this text.

Finally, as an example of the degree of perfection in design now

---

[75] *H.* iii 1934, 3-4, 5.
[76] Not impossible, however, if the mason's eye had slipped. He could well have decided just to carry on with the lunar day once he had realised his mistake.
[77] *Calendars of Athens*, p. 53.
[78] See 'Αρχ. 'Εφ. 107 1968 (pub. 1969), 108-115.
[79] Interpretating the disputed letter as sigma: see *TAY* p. 100.
[80] 'Αρχ. 'Εφ. 107 1968 (pub. 1969), p. 115.

achieved by the end of this period, consider ii²373, an honorary decree for Euenor of Akarnania, 322/1:[81]

stoichedon 39

['Επ]ὶ Φιλοκλέους ἄρχοντος ἐπὶ τῆς Οἰνεῖδος ἐνά[τ]
[ης] πρυτανείας ἧι Εὐθυγένης Ἡφαιστοδήμου Κηφι[σ]
[ιε]ύς ἐγραμμάτευεν· Θαργηλιῶνος δευτέραι ἱστα
[μέ]νου, τρίτει καὶ εἰκοστεῖ τῆς πρυτανείας· ἐκκ[λ]
[ησ]ία· τῶν προέδρων ἐπεψήφιζεν Εὔαλκος Φαληρε[ύ]
[ς· ἔ]δοξεν τῶι δήμωι· Διόφαντος Φρασικλείδου Μυ[ρ]
[ρι]νούσιος εἶπεν·

---

[81] Cf. *TAY* p. 111.

CHAPTER FOUR

THE YEARS 321 TO 291 [1]

A. *The anagrapheis*

I begin this chapter with an examination of two small series of inscriptions in which the recording officer is the anagrapheus,[2] not the usual γραμματεὺς κατὰ πρυτανείαν. During the years represented by these two groups we find forms of non-democratic government in Athens: 321/0-319/18, the years between the occupation of the Piraeus by a Macedonian garrison in late summer 322 and the restoration of the democracy in the first half of 318, were a period of oligarchic control, when the franchise was limited to 9,000 of the 21,000 citizens; [3] 294/3-292/1 involve the so-called 'dictatorship' of Olympiodoros, who held an unconstitutional two-year archonship, and the following year. Thus in six years—and only six—we find the anagrapheus as a prominent official in the superscripts and prescripts of decrees.

There were, moreover, as the evidence clearly shows, 'democratic' [4] anagrapheis, but they were probably minor officials with clerical duties in the Metroon.[5] During the two brief periods dealt with here, however, the anagrapheis rose to prominence and assumed the duty of publishing the decrees of the boule and ecclesia, while the successive prytany secretaries, previously entrusted with this task, lost their annual status as well, being chosen for limited periods of one prytany from among the members of the prytanising tribe.

Although these two periods are separated from each other by some 26 years, I have, for reasons that are obvious, chosen to treat them here together. The number of documents involved

[1] Some 85 documents are available as evidence for this period.

[2] For full background information and bibliography see S. Dow, "The Athenian Anagrapheis," *HSCP* lxvii 1963, 38-54 (abbreviated 'Dow' in the table below). See also B. D. Meritt, "The Year of Neaichmos," *H.* xxxii 1963, 425-438 (abbreviated 'Meritt' in the table below).

[3] See W. S. Ferguson, *Hellenistic Athens*, 19-26.

[4] I.e. officials of 'democratic' years in the second half of the fourth century and the first two decades of the third.

[5] So W. S. Ferguson, *The Athenian Secretaries*, Cornell Univ. Studies in Class. Philology n. vii 1898, p. 41.

is in total relatively small (especially for the later period) and decrees recorded by anagrapheis are so much *sui generis* that it seems both expedient and advantageous to treat them as a single body. In order to facilitate understanding of the formulations employed to incorporate the anagrapheus at the head of the decree and also to provide an up-to-date record of the assignation of the various inscriptions to particular years I present the evidence first in tabular form, see pages 52-53.[6]

The following points should be noticed:

(1) Superscripts:[7] θεοί appears 8 times, a frequency not unexpected, normally in first position. In one instance only the anagrapheus is placed before θεοί: ii²383b (Add. p. 660) (*S.* xxi 305), 320/19:

> ['Αναγ]ραφεύ[ς 'Αρχέδικος Ναυκρίτου Λαμπτρεύς].
> Θ ε [ο ί]
> 'Επὶ Νεαίχμ[ου ἄρχοντος ἐπὶ τῆς] stoichedon 25

The honorand is named superscript on 4 occasions, by himself in the nominative (?) (*S.* xxi 306a, 320/19) and in the genitive (ii²385a [*S.* xxi 355], 292/1), and twice with πολιτεία (+ dative) (*S.* xxi 310 and ii²386, *c.* Add. p. 660 [*S.* xxi 311], 319/18).

As for the anagrapheus—the only official to appear superscript in these documents and only, as far as the evidence goes, in the first period—[8] the formulation for the three (or four) extant examples is always in the sequence anagrapheus + name. Except in 319/18, when, as we shall see, the anagrapheus never has his patronymic, the patronymic is otherwise expressed.[9]

(2) Prescripts: opening formulae: Dow[10] attempted to divide

[6] In column 4 'S/P' indicates whether the anagrapheus appears superscript or as part of the prescript. In column 6 'NPD' = *nomen-patronymicum-demoticum*.

[7] I count as superscript any anagrapheus who appears in a superior position divorced from the prescript proper. Thus e.g. *S.* xxi 310, 319/18, where the *vacat* at the end of v. 3 suggests that the anagrapheus strictly belongs with the preceding items rather than the following prescript.

[8] Evidence for the second period is so slight that one hesitates to make any sort of generalisation. It appears, however, that under Olympiodorus superscripts were dispensed with.

[9] Anagrapheus + NPD: ii²380, 320/19; and restored in ii²546 (*S.* xxi 304), 321/0 and ii²383b, Add. p. 660 (*S.* xxi 305), 320/19; anagrapheus ND: *S.* xxi 310, 319/18.

[10] *HSCP* lxvii 1963, 38-54.

Inscriptions recorded by anagrapheis

Text	Number of Prytany	Superscript	S/P	Secretary	Opening formulae	Items omitted	References
		321/0: *anagrapheus—Thrasykles son of Nausikrates of Thria*; *archon — Archippos*					
S. xxi 303	V	[θε]οί	P	Σωκράτης Εὐμάχου Εὐπυρίδης	ἀναγραφεὺς NPD, ἐπὶ Ἀρχίππου ἄρχοντος		Dow 44-5; id. *H.* xxxii 1963, 344-5; Meritt *ibid.* 430-1.
ii²546 (*S.* xxi 304)	?	[anagrapheus]	[S]	Ἀριστ...... ....17.....	do.		Meritt *H.* xxx 1961, 290; Dow *H.* xxxii 1963, 351.
		320/19: *anagrapheus — Archedikos son of Naukritos of Lamptrai*; *archon — Neaichmos*					
ii²380	II	anagrapheus	S	Θηραμένης Κηφισιεύς	ἀναγραφεὺς NPD, ἐπὶ Νεαίχμου ἄρχοντος		*TAY* p. 113; Dow 45.
ii²381	V	none	P	Νικόδημος Ἀναφλύστιος	do.		*TAY* p. 118; Dow 45-6.
ii²382 (*c.* Add. p. 660)	V	[θε]ο[ί]	P	[Νικόδημος Ἀναφλύστιος]	do.		*TAY* p. 118; Dow 46.
S. xxi 306a	[VI]	honorand	P	..νων Ὀῆθεν	ἐπὶ Νεαίχμου ἄρχοντος, ἀναγραφέως δὲ NPD		Dow *HSCP* lxvii 1963, 74; Meritt 425-432.
ii²383b (Add. p. 660) (*S.* xxi 305)	[VII]	anagrapheus θε[οί]	S	Στρατωνίδης Παιανιεύς	ἀναγραφεὺς NPD, θεοί, ἐπὶ Νεαίχμου ἄρχοντος	name of month	Dow *ibid.* 60-7; Meritt *AJP* xciii 1972, 167-8.
H. xl 174-5, 25	X	none	P	probably omitted	ἀναγραφεὺς NPD, ἐπὶ Νεαίχμου ἄρχοντος	?secretary, month	Meritt *ibid.* 166-7.
ii²383	[X]	[θε]οί	P	. ψι[- - - - -]	do.	?	Meritt *ibid.* 166-8; Dow 46.
ii²384 (*S.* xxi 309)	?	θ[εοί]	P	?	?do.	?	Dow 46.
		319/18: *anagrapheus — Eukadmos of Anakaia (no patronymic)*; *archon — Apollodoros.*					
S. xxi 310	IV	Θεοί. Πολιτεία Αἰνήτωι Ῥοδίωι.	S	none	ἀναγραφεὺς ND, ἐπὶ Ἀπολλοδώρου ἄρχοντος	secretary	*TAY* pp. 121-2; Dow 47.

ii²386 (*c. Add.* p. 660) (*S.* xxi 311)	VI	Θεοί Πολιτεία Ἀμυντ ...c.8...	P	?Ạ[..]ι[- -] ?Ạ[..]ι[- -]	ἐπὶ Ἀπολλοδώρου ἄρχοντος, ἐπὶ τῆς Αἰγεῖδος ἕκτης πρυτανείας· [γραμματεὺς ND, ἀναγραφεὺς ND]		*TAY* p. 122; Dow 47-9.
S. xxi 312	VII	none	P	none	ἐπὶ Ἀπολλοδώρου ἄρχοντος, ἐπὶ τῆς Ἀντιοχίδος ἑβδόμης πρυτανείας καὶ ἀναγραφέως ND		*TAY* p. 122; Dow 49.
ii²388	VIII	none	P	Φιλοκτήμων Κηφισιεύς	ἐπὶ Ἀπολλοδώρου ἄρχοντος καὶ ἀναγραφέως ND	?	*TAY* pp. 122-3; Dow 49; *S.* xxi 313.
ii²387	X	none	P	Ἀφόβητος Κοθωκίδης	as in ii²386	see below	*TAY* p. 123; Dow 49-50; *S.* xxi 314.
ii²390 (*TAY* p. 123)	X	[Θ]ε[οί]	P	none	ἐπὶ ἀναγραφέως ND καὶ Ἀπολλοδώρου ἄρχοντος	?secretary	Dow 50; *S.* xxi 315.
S. xxi 316	[X]	none	P	none	ἐπὶ Ἀπολλοδώρου ἄρχοντος, ἀναγραφέως δὲ ND	secretary	*TAY* p. 124; Dow 50.
294/3: ***anagrapheus* — *Thras - - - of Phyle*; *archon* — *Olympiodoros*.**							
ii²378 (*S.* xxi 353B)	[VI]	none	P	none	Ἄρχων Ὀλυμπιόδωρος· ἐπὶ ἀναγραφέως NPD	secretary	Dow *H.* xxxii 1963, 345-6; Meritt *ibid.* 429-431.
293/2:[11] ***anagrapheus* — *Epikouros son of Epiteles of Rhamnous*; *archon* — *Olympiodoros*.**							
ii²389 (*S.* xxi 354)	[XI]	none	P	none	ἐπὶ Ὀλυμπιοδώρου ἄρχοντος δεύτερον ἔτος, ἀναγραφέως δὲ NPD	secretary	Dow 51; id. *H.* xxxii 1963, 346-7.
ii²649 (Dinsmoor *AA* 7-8)	<XI>	none	P	none	ἐπὶ Ὀλυμπιοδώρου ἄρχοντος, ἀναγραφέως δὲ NPD	secretary	Dow 51.
H. vii 97-100, 17	XI	none	P	none	do.	secretary	Dow 51.
292/1: ***anagrapheus* — *Th- - - of Oion*; *archon* — *Philippos*.**							
ii²385a (*S.* xxi 355)	?	[?Αριστο]νίκου	P	?none	?ἐπὶ Φιλίππου ἄρχοντος, ἀναγραφέως δὲ NPD	?	Dow 51-3.

[11] All three texts of this year were passed on the same day. The prytany was the eleventh (not X, as in Dow 51).

the evidence for the anagrapheis into various types according to the formulations adopted in expressing the item. Unfortunately, his category II does not seem to exist; [12] nor does he admit of the type with the archon in the nominative.[13] Rather than compound the confusion I offer the following analysis based primarily on whether the anagrapheus appears in the nominative or in the genitive:

Type I: ἀναγραφεύς in nominative [14]

a) ἀναγραφεύς NPD (superscript), followed by a prescript commencing with ἐπὶ N. ἄρχοντος:

?*S*. xxi 304, 321/0; ii²380, ii²383b (Add. p. 660) (*S*. xxi 305), 320/19; *S*. xxi 310 (ND only), 319/18.

b) ἀναγραφεύς NPD as first item in the prescript, followed by ἐπὶ N. ἄρχοντος:

S. xxi 303, 321/0; ii²381 and 382, *H*. xl 174-5, 25, ii²383, ?ii²384 (*S*. xxi 309), all 320/19.

c) ἐπὶ N. ἄρχοντος, ἐπὶ τῆς N. ordinal πρυτανείας· γραμματεύς ND, ἀναγραφεύς ND:

?ii²386, *c*. Add. p. 660 (*S*. xxi 311), and ii²387, both 319/18.

Type II: ἀναγραφεύς combined with the archon formula (in genitive)

a) ἐπὶ N. ἄρχοντος, ἀναγραφέως δὲ NPD:

S. xxi 306a, 320/19; *S*. xxi 316 (ND only), 319/18; ii²389 (*S*. xxi 354),[15] ii²649 (Dinsmoor *AA* pp. 7-8), *H*. vii 97-100, 17, all 293/2; ?ii²385a (*S*. xxi 355), 292/1.

b) ἐπὶ N. ἄρχοντος καὶ [16] ἀναγραφέως ND:

ii²388, 319/18.

Cf. ἐπὶ N. ἄρχοντος, ἐπὶ τῆς N. ordinal πρυτανείας καὶ ἀναγραφέως ND:

---

[12] See Meritt, *H*. xxxii 1963, 429-30.

[13] *Art. cit.*, p. 53.

[14] My Ia + b = Dow's Type I.

[15] We find a slight variation here in that a reference to the fact that this is Olympiodoros' second year is added: ['Επὶ 'Ολυμπ]ιοδώρου ἄρχοντος δεύτε[ρον ἔτ]|[ος: it may well be that ii²389 was the first of the three texts of this day to be inscribed; in the other two the anagrapheus did not trouble to qualify the year.

[16] All three examples with καί have been restored, but, it appears, correctly.

S. xxi 312, 319/18, which may well be a mere erroneous version of the formulation in which the anagrapheus comes immediately after ἄρχοντος (with καί).[17]

Type III: ἄρχων N followed by ἐπὶ ἀναγραφέως NPD: ii²378 (*S*. xxi 353B), 294/3.

This type is not recognised by Dow.[18] Meritt's parallels, however, for formulations with the archon in the nominative are indisputable: ii²658, 283/2:

["Α]ρχων Εὔθιος· ἐπὶ τῆς Δημητρι|[άδ]ο[ς κτλ.

and *S*. xxv 90, 281/0:

"Αρχων Οὐρίας· ἐπὶ τῆς Αἰαντίδο[ς κτλ.

Clearly, as one would expect with so little evidence from such a short period, the picture is one of great variety. However, there is no question but that the two most popular formulations are Types I a and b and Type IIa. Further than that the evidence is insufficient to take us, although we might note once again that, as in the case of superscripts, so too here the word ἀναγραφεύς always precedes the name.

(3) The secretaries: As we have already noted, during the ascendancy of the anagrapheis the secretaries reverted to the system whereby they changed with each prytany. Clear evidence of this is found in the three years of the first period, where the secretaries are included in the prescript more often than not.[19] It is an interesting reflection on their decreased status that, even when included, they never have the patronymic, except in the first year (321/0), where the secretary's patronymic is to be restored in *S*. xxi 303, and possibly also in ii²546 (*S*. xxi 304). Dow [20] notes that the secretary always appears immediately after the phrase for the prytany (of which, of course, he was a member).[21]

---

[17] Note that ii²388 and *S*. xxi 312 belong to successive prytanies of the same year.

[18] *Art. cit.*, p. 53.

[19] The evidence (such as it is) suggests that in the second period the secretary was never included. (Note that Down's claim, *art. cit.*, pp. 46-7, that secretaries are always named in the year 320/19 is now open to dispute: *H*. xl 174-5, 25 is best restored *without* a secretary: see Meritt *AJP* xciii 1972, 166-7.)

[20] *Art. cit.*, p. 54.

[21] For the unusual ii²387 see 6) below.

(4) Lunar date: In ii^{2}383b, Add. p. 660 (*S.* xxi 305) the name of the month is omitted, although the day is given. A more significant anomaly is ii^{2}546 (*S.* xxi 304), where the day of the month *precedes* the name of the month:

[. . . . ἐγραμμ]άτευε· δεκάτει ὑ[στέραι . . . 7 . . .] stoichedon 36
. . . . . 11 . . . . . καὶ δεκάτει τῆ[ς πρυτανείας·

Even this is not unparalleled: cf. ii^{2}351 + 624 (Tod 198), 330/29.[22]

(5) Type of meeting: Note *S.* xxi 312, 319/18, where we read (vv. 6-7):

ἐ̣[κκ]λ̣[η]σία κατὰ ψ[ήφ] stoichedon 26
ισμα βουλῆς·

For this formulation cf. ii^{2}554, ?307-4, which has been restored to read:

ἐκκλησία κατὰ ψήφισ] stoichedon 23
μα δήμου·[23]

(6) ii^{2}387, 319/18: This prescript requires special consideration:[24]

['Επὶ 'Απολλοδώ]ρου ἄ[ρχοντο] stoichedon 21 (vv. 1-2)
[ς ἐπὶ τῆς δεκά]της π[ρυτανε]
[ίας· γραμματεὺ]ς 'Αφόβητο[ς Κο] stoichedon 23 (vv. 3-16)
[θωκίδης· ἀναγρ]αφεὺς Εὔκα[δμ]
[ος 'Ανακαιεύς· Κ]τησίας Χιω[νί]
[δου . . . . 9 . . . .]ος εἶπεν·

This prescript is remarkable in many ways: it offers a virtually unique format and sequence for the items for secretary and anagrapheus; moreover, several items are entirely omitted—lunar and conciliar dating, type of meeting, chairman of the proedroi, and the enactment formula; nor is the *name* of the prytany recorded. No other prescript of these two groups is so deficient, and the only possible parallel is the extremely fragmentary ii^{2}386, Add. p. 660 (*S.* xxi 311) of the same year, for which a similar structure has been suggested.

---

[22] See pp. 46-47 above.
[23] See also p. 72 below
[24] See *S.* xxi 314 and Dow, *art. cit.*, pp. 49-50.

Dow described this year (319/18) as "a year of variety, perhaps confusion," [25] an observation which ii²387 goes some way to confirming.

Conclusion

In the case of the anagrapheis then we have a limited phenomenon which suddenly appears with considerable impact—no doubt, as Dow observes, reflecting the underlying changes in the form of government at Athens. The new official achieves remarkable prominence, indicating his status in the secretariat real or assumed. Until this official comes upon the scene, the archon's now established primacy in prescripts is unchallenged: but in the new set-up on only one occasion down to the end of 320/19 does the archon not yield pride of place to the anagrapheus.

It does seem, however, that powerful though this new official may have been, the first flush of secretarial dominance did not last. By 319/18 his prominence is on the wane: he has lost (or discarded) the patronymic and politely deferred, in 5 cases out of 7, to the archon. On two occasions indeed in that year we find him much further down the list.

During the second period of his activity it is difficult to generalise, but even from the primacy of the archon it seems reasonable to conclude that the anagrapheus did not regain the status [26] his predecessors held 26 years before. The explanation for this apparent differentiation between the two periods may lie in the fact that, whereas in 321/0-319/18 the regime was unashamedly oligarchic, in the late 290s the constitution was, at least nominally, democratic.

B. *From 318/17 to 295/4*

We turn now to the years intervening between the two periods of anagrapheis, first to the brief democratic interlude between the end of the oligarchy in 319/18 and the beginning of the regime of Demetrios of Phaleron sometime after prytany VI of 318/17. For this short period we have only four prescripts,[27] of which the most significant feature is the reappearance of the secretary of the

---

[25] *Art. cit.*, p. 50.

[26] Although he appears to have regained his patronymic.

[27] ii²448 II, of the fourth prytany; ii²535 (*S.* xxi 318) and *S.* xxi 319, both probably of the same day of the sixth prytany; and ii²350 (*S.* xxi 320), probably of the seventh prytany. (See Meritt, *H.* xliii 1974, 463-5 and xlv 1976, 173).

Council, a clear reflection of underlying democratic procedures. There is little else worthy of comment, apart from some minor anomalies in ii^{2}448 II and ii^{2}350 (*S.* xxi 320).[28]

Soon, however, power was in the hands of Kassandros' regent, Demetrios of Phaleron, whose regime, though professedly democratic, was in reality a form of tyranny.[29] Very few decrees [30] indeed seem to have been published during the years of his control (318/17-308/7), but they all have one feature in common, again reflecting the form of government, in that the secretary is completely absent from the prescript.[31] Apart from one instance of omission of the enactment formula [32] and a possible example of the month in the genitive without specification of the day,[33] there is little that is otherwise remarkable about the three securely dated inscriptions.

ii^{2}449, however, deserves closer attention: [34]

[Ἐ]πὶ τῆς Αἰαντίδ[ος ἕκτης πρυτ] stoichedon 24
[α]νείας· ὀγδόηι [ἐπὶ δέκα, ἕκτηι]
τῆς πρυτανείας· [ἐκκλησία· τῶν]
προέδρων ἐπεψή[φιζεν . . .^{6}. . .]
.ς Λαμπτρεύς· συν[πρόεδροι· κτλ.

This prescript is manifestly deficient, a deficiency explained away, according to Koehler, by assuming that a second decree of the same year stood higher on the stone. This could account for the absence of the archon, but not for the omission of the name of the month.

The dearth of epigraphical material from the period of Demetrios of Phaleron is more than compensated for by the sudden flood [35]

---

[28] The enactment formula is omitted in both, while in the former we find the form ἐπεψήφισζε in the epistates item.

[29] Cf. H. Berve, *Die Tyrannis bei den Griechen*, I, 326-7.

[30] ii^{2}450, 314/13; ii^{2}451, 313/12; ii^{2}453, 310/09; and probably also ii^{2}449, 317-307.

[31] Cf. PM p. 7: "With so little evidence about the decade of Demetrios of Phaleron it is impossible to say much about the secretaries of the Council during his régime, but our belief is that they were of minor importance, not named in decrees, and that they probably were not annual officers." See also *ibid.*, note 24.

[32] ii^{2}450, 314/13.

[33] ii^{2}451, 313/12.

[34] See *S.* xxi 325.

[35] Some 14 prescripts of the year of Anaxikrates have survived: Prytany I - *S.* xxi 334; IV - ii^{2}464; V - ii^{2}456; VII - ii^{2}458; IX - ii^{2}459 (*S.* xxv 77);

of documents for the year 307/6:[36] this clearly reflects the political situation, that is to say the restitution of democratic procedures by Demetrios Poliorketes late in the year 308/7. As is to be expected, the annual secretary of the Council resumes his place in prescripts.[37]

We are fortunate enough to have extant a decree from the eleventh day of 307/6. It is extremely fragmentary but enough remains to show that the 'democratic form' was already back in use: *S.* xxi 334:

['Επὶ 'Αναξικράτους ἄρχ]οντος ἐπὶ [τ] stoichedon 27
[ῆς . . . . 10 . . . . πρώτης] πρυ[τ]ανε[ία]
[ς ἧι Λυσίας Νοθίππου Δ]ιο[μ]ει[εὺς ἐ]
[γραμμάτευεν. 'Εκατομ]βα[ιῶ]νος [ἑνδ]
[εκάτει, ἐνδεκάτει τῆς] πρυταν[εία]
[ς· ἐκκλησία κυρία· τῶν] προέδρω[ν ἐπ]
[εψήφιζεν - - - - - - - - - - - - -] *vacat*
- - - - - - - - - - - - - - - - - - - *v* ἔδοξε[ν τῶ]
[ι δήμωι· . . . . . 12 . . . . .]οστράτ[ου.]
[. . . 7 . . . εἶπεν·

Although the series of documents of 307/6 is of great interest and importance to students of the calendar, there is little that requires particular comment as regards the format of the prescripts. In the following list of minor details I have therefore included evidence for all the years down to 295/4 as well:

(1) Superscripts: The general trend away from superscripts seems to be maintained.[38] ii^{2}358 (*S.* xxi 326), 307/6, however, is interesting in that we find there the archon formula in larger letters across the top of the stone; cf. also ii^{2}463 of the same year, where the archon and the enactment formula are similarly spread across the width of the stone.[39]

X - ii^{2}461, 462, *S.* iii 86, ii^{2}358 (*S.* xxi 326); XI - ii^{2}455 (*S.* xxi 327); XII - ii^{2}460 (*S.* xxi 331): also ii^{2}457, 463, 465.

[36] For the chronology of 307/6 see Meritt, *H.* xxxiii 1964, 13-15.

[37] Although he appears to be absent in ii^{2}459 (*S.* xxv 77), as well as in the curtailed prescripts ii^{2}457 and 463. Cf. also ii^{2}472 + 169 (Add. p. 661), 306/5, and ii^{2}646, 295/4 (for this last text see now Traill, *H.* Suppl. xiv p. 131).

[38] Apart from several instances of θεοί, we find some examples of the honorand in this position: ii^{2}459 (*S.* xxv 77) and *S.* iii 86, 307/6; ii^{2}797 (*S.* xxi 337), 305/4; *S.* xvi 58, 304/3; ii^{2}494, 303/2.

[39] The *Corpus* text does not give an accurate indication of how vs. 1 is cut right across the full width.

(2) Archon formula: This is slightly adjusted in 296/5 to reflect the political situation. The archon Nikias did not assume office until the tyranny of Lachares was overthrown in the spring of 295: ii^{2}644 (*TAY* p. 179): [40]

'Επὶ Νικίου ἄρχοντος ὑστέρ[ου ἐπὶ] stoichedon 27
τῆς 'Ακαμ[α]ντίδος τετάρτης π[ρυτα]
[νε]ίας·

(3) Secretary without patronymic: *S.* xviii 16, 302/1 is restored to give a secretary with name and demotic only:

'Επὶ Νικοκλέους [ἄρχοντος ἐπ] stoichedon 23
ὶ τῆς Κεκροπίδο[ς πέμπτης πρ]
[υτα]νείας ἧι Νίκ[ων Πλωθεεὺς]
[ἐγραμ]μάτευεν· Μα[ιμακτηριῶ]
[νος ἑβδ]όμε[ι. . . . . .^{13}. . . . . .]
. . .^{7}. . . τ . . . . . ο . . . .^{9}. . . .

In contrast there are 8 other prescripts of this year all offering secretaries with both patronymic and demotic.[41]

(4) Dating formulae: The month appears in the genitive, without specification of the day, in ii^{2}464, 307/6 (as restored) and *H.* iii 5-6, 6, 306/5; the name of the month is omitted in ii^{2}500, 302/1; and the prytany date is omitted in *S.* iii 86.[42] More significantly, we find in 307/6—and in that year alone—[43] two examples of the expression ἡμερολεγδόν: ii^{2}458, the one and only sure occurrence: (vv. 4-7)

Γαμηλιῶν stoichedon 25
ος δευτ[έ]ραι ἐ[μ]βολίμωι, ὀγδόε[ι]
μετ' εἰκάδας ἡμερολεγδόν, μιᾶ[ι]
καὶ εἰκοστεῖ τῆς πρυτανε[ίας·

The scribe appears to be drawing attention to the fact that a day

[40] So too ii^{2}645 of the same year.
[41] ii^{2}500-505; *H.* v 414-6, 12; *H.* ix 104-11, 20.
[42] Altogether an unusual document.
[43] According to Meritt, 'Αρχ. 'Εφ. 107, 1968 (pub. 1969), 108-115, who argues (convincingly) that ἡμερολεγδόν was an expression peculiar to the scribe of 307/6 and used by him for the purpose of naming days with more than one intercalation, as a means of clarifying the resulting cumbersome terminology.

really the 24th was called the 22nd plus 2.[44] Cf. ii^{2}459 (*S*. xxv 77) where the expression is also certainly to be restored: (vv. 2-3):

stoichedon 50

'Ανθẹ[στηριῶνος ἑνδεκάτει τετάρτει ἐμβολίμωι ἡμερολ]
[εγδό]ν, ὀγδ[όει τῆς πρυτανείας·

Here Anthesterion 15 is expressed as Anthesterion 11 intercalated for the fourth time: in fact the real date is Anthesterion 20, for the assumption underlying this equation is that Anthesterion 11 was itself already retarded by 5 days.[45]

(5) Enactment formula: [46] Apart from the omission of the enactment formula in ii^{2}460 and *S*. iii 86, both of 307/6 and in ii^{2}500, 302/1, note the appearance ot the formula in first position (as in old style) in ii^{2}456 (PM pp. 12-13), 307/6:

stoichedon 41

["Εδοξεν τῆι βουλῆι καὶ τῶι δ]ήμωι· ἐπὶ 'Αναξικράτους
[ἄρχοντος,

(6) Orator without patronymic or demotic: ii^{2}598, *fin.s.*iv, appears to offer an example of the orator with name alone:

[- - - - - K]τησίας εἶπεν·

This is so unexpected that I feel there is no other explanation than to assume that this text is not a state document.[47]

(7) Curtailed prescripts: In two cases of the year 307/6 we find extremely abbreviated prescripts consisting apparently only of archon, enactment formula and orator: [48]
ii^{2}457, an honorary decree:

stoichedon 42

['Επὶ 'Αναξικράτους ἄρχοντ]ος· ἔδοξεν τῶι δήμωι· Στρατ
[οκλῆς Εὐθυδήμου Διομεεύ]ς εἶπεν·

---

[44] Although, as Meritt points out, no explanation was felt necessary in the case of *S*. xiv 65, 271/0, where the date Elaphebolion 13 was called Elaphebolion 9 plus 4, or in the case of ii^{2}864 (*S*. xxi 429), 181/0, where a date which should have been Metageitnion 3 was called Hekatombaion 25 plus 8.

[45] See Meritt, *art. cit.*, p. 114.

[46] For the emphasising of the enactment formula see below, p. 63.

[47] Perhaps tribal or demotic. The prescripts of non-state documents did not, of course, contain all the canonical elements of their state counterparts.

[48] Cf. ii^{2}107 (Tod 131), vv. 35-7, 369/8, page 32 above.

ii^{2}463, decree on rebuilding of the Long Walls: [49]

['Επὶ 'Αναξικράτους ἄρχοντος· ἔδο]ξεν τῶ[ι] δήμω[ι]·
[Δημοχάρης Λάχητος Λευκονοιεὺς εἶπεν· stoichedon 71

cf. also ii^{2}467, 306/5, where we seem to have only archon, prytanising tribe and orator:

['Επὶ] Κοροίβου ἄρχοντ[ος ἐπὶ τῆς . . . . . . 14 . . . . . .] stoichedon 39
[.ς π]ρυτανείας. *vacat*
Διότιμος Διοπείθου [Εὐωνυμεὺς εἶπεν·

(8) Unusual prescript: The most unusual prescript of this period is *S*. iii 86, 307/6: [50]

[Πριην]εῦσι *vvvv* Μακαρεῖ Λ[υκωπάδου],
[Μνησέα]ι Ἑκατομβίου, *vv* Ἡγ' ---
['Επὶ] 'Ạṿạξικράτους ἄρ[χοντος, κατὰ τὸ ψήφισ]
[μα τ]οῦ δήμου, ἐπὶ τῆς [Ἱ]πποθ̣[ωντίδος δεκάτης πρ]
[υτα]ṿείας εἶ Λυσίας Νοθ[ίππου Διομεεὺς ἐγρα]
[μμά]τευεν· 'Ελαφηβολιῶṿ[ος ---- ἱσταμένου·]
[Στρ]ατοκλῆς Εὐθυδήμου [Διομεεὺς εἶπεν·

with its impressive superscript, and lack of prytany date, epistates and enactment formula. In particular, the restoration of vv. 1-2 must raise some doubts. Hondius himself adduced ii^{2}1487, a *traditio* of the Treasurers of Athena and the Other Gods, where in vv. 53-5 we read:

ἐπ' 'Αναξικρ[άτους ἄρχοντος --- Γ]
αμηλιῶνος ὑστ[έρου --- κατὰ τὸ ψήφισ]
μα τοῦ δήμο[υ δ -------- εἶπεν·]

But this is hardly a parallel: ii^{2}1487 is not a prescript to a decree but merely a heading to an item in a *traditio*. Nor are *S*. xxi 312, 319/18 and ii^{2}554, *fin.s.* iv (?307-4) [51] strictly parallels, since both of them involve formulae relevant to the meeting of the ecclesia.[52] ii^{2}77, ?*ante* 378/7 is perhaps closer: ἔδ]|οξεν [τῆ]ι βουλῆι κατὰ τὸ

[49] V. 1 is spread out across the width of the stone.

[50] See J. J. E. Hondius, *Novae Inscriptiones Atticae*, 1925, 39-40 n. V, and pp. 42-3.

[51] For the date see *H*. xxxii 1963, 4.

[52] ẹ[κκ]λ̣[η]σία κατὰ ψ[ήφ]|ισμα βουλῆς, *S*. xxi 312, vv. 6-7; ἐκκλησία κατὰ ψήφισ]|μα δήμου ii^{2}554 vv. 1-2 (the opening lines of this prescript are lacking). Note that ii^{2}462 is no longer to be restored in a similar way: see Meritt, *H*. xxxii 1963, 437.

το[ῦ δήμου ψήφισμα],[53] especially in view of the position in which the formula occurs. It may well be that *S.* iii 86 is a decree of the boule and that the enactment formula should have been expressed immediately after the archon. There seems no other way to justify the phrase κατὰ τὸ ψήφισμα τοῦ δήμου.[54]

(9) Uninscribed spaces:[55] Now that the sequence of items in the prescript had become more or less rigid, there was no real way in the solid block of letters to denote special emphasis save by isolating or setting off an item by leaving an uninscribed area before or after it. One item which had always been felt to be of cardinal importance was the enactment formula. In Chapter III we had occasion to comment on the stubbornness with which the enactment formula managed to retain something of its original primacy by appearing —often on its own—in a new line, as if thus at the beginning of a prescript,[56] or by interrupting an apparently new style prescript to initiate an old style sequence.[57] This phenomenon is further illustrated by texts of the period under discussion e.g. ii^{2}456, 307/6, enactment formula in first position; ii^{2}463, 307/6, enactment formula, with archon, in larger letters across the width of the stone.

A second item which also achieved emphasis in a similar way was the orator,[58] first in ii^{2}209, 349/8:

['Επὶ Καλλιμάχου ἄρχ]οντος· ἔδοξεν τῶι δήμ   stoichedon 33
[ωι· . . . ^{7} . . .ις ἐπρυτ]άνευε, Διεύχης Δημάρ
[χο Φρεάρριος ἐγραμ]μάτευε· τῶν προέδρων
[ἐπεψήφιζε . . . . ^{8} . . . .]δης Γαργήττιος· *vvv*
['Ιεροκλείδης Τιμοσ]τράτου 'Αλωπεκῆθεν *v*
[εἶπεν·

[53] Vv. 1-2: cf. vv. 9-10, and see above p. 33.

[54] "eiusmodi omissiones et inconstantiae, quae in titulis anni 307/6 complures occurrunt, haud scio an turbido Atheniensium rei publicae statui imputandae sint," Hondius, *op. cit.*, p. 43.

[55] See W. B. Dinsmoor, *The Athenian Archon List in the Light of Recent Discoveries* 1939, 14-18, following Dow, *AJA* xl 1936, 62-66. ("Design in Preambles of Decrees").

[56] Pp. 28-30 above.

[57] P. 30 above.

[58] J. Bingen, *Le Monde Grec* (*Hommages à Claire Préaux*) 1975, 470-9, sees this not as emphasis of the mover-item but as a clear indication that the Athenians associated the mover with the following motion, rather than with the preceding 'références'.

Before this time the orator had never been raised to any prominence, but it seems that, when the leading politicians themselves (rather than their mouthpieces) began to propose measures in the assembly, their importance was recognised and reflected in the emphasis given to the orator's name in prescripts. This emphasis could be achieved by placing the orator at the beginning of a line, usually by leaving space uninscribed at the end of the previous line: e.g. *S.* xxi 288, 327/6: [59]

τ] stoichedon 33
[ῶν προέδρων ἐπεψή]φιζεν Πάμφιλος Π[αιαν]
[ιεύς· ἔδοξεν τῶι δή]μωι· *vacat*
. . . . .17. . . . . Θριά[σ]ιος εἶπ[εν·

A similar prominence for the orator is also achieved in *mid-line* by leaving uninscribed space between the enactment formula and the orator's name: e.g. ii^{2}448 I, 323/2:

ἔδοξεν] stoichedon 41
τῶι δήμωι· *vv* Εὐφίλητος Εὐφι̣[λ]ή[του Κηφισιεὺς εἶπε]
ν·

The most impressive example of this style is perhaps ii^{2}498, 303/2, where 6 uninscribed spaces are left in mid-line: vv. 8-10:

ἔδοξεν τῆι βουλε stoichedon 29
[ῖ κ]αὶ τῶι δήμωι· *vvvvvv* Φιλόστρατος
[Φ]ιλοστράτου Κηφισιεὺς εἶπεν· [60]

In two instances, however, we should note that the uninscribed space is left *before the enactment formula*: ii^{2}486, 304/3, vv. 8-11:

τῶν προέδρων ἐπεψ[ήφιζεν Εὐχθόνιος] stoichedon 33
'Επιμηδείδου Κυδαθη[ναιεὺς καὶ συμπρόε]
δροι· *vvvv* ἔδοξεν τῶι [δήμωι· Στρατοκλῆς Ε]
ὐθυδήμου Διομεεὺς [εἶπεν·

---

[59] Cf. also ii^{2}548, between *c.* 330 and 308/7; ii^{2}372, 322/1 (Demades); ii^{2}374, *c.* 320; *S.* xxi 310 and 312, 319/18; ii^{2}358 (*S.* xxi 326) and ii^{2}455, 307/6; ii^{2}504, 302/1. In ii^{2}360, 325/4, where the enactment formula is omitted, the demotic of the (now immediately) preceding epistates is abbreviated ('Ελευσί·) to allow the orator (Demosthenes) to stand right at the beginning of the following line.

[60] Cf. also: 3 uninscribed spaces—*H.* iii 5-6, 6, 306/5; 2 uninscribed spaces—ii^{2}554, *fin.s.* iv (?307-4); *H.* ix 104-11, 20, 302/1; 1 uninscribed space—ii^{2}471, 306/5; *S.* xvi 58, 304/3.

and in ii^{2}493, 303/2, vv. 8-12:

τῶν προέδρων ἐπ — stoichedon 26
εψήφιζεν Δεξίμβροτος Ἀρκεσίλ
ου Παιανιεὺς καὶ συμπρόεδροι· *v*
ἔδοξεν τῶι δήμωι· Καλλίας Λυσιμ
άχου Ἕρμειος εἶπεν·

The natural assumption here is that it is the enactment formula which is being given the emphasis. Indeed, this would seem to be the first step towards Dow's 'perfect design',[61] in which the enactment formula is centred in a line by itself.[62] By this simple device the enactment formula is conspicuously placed in such a position as to separate the prescript from the text of the decree: moreover, the orator too receives his share of the limelight by 'naming', as it were, the decree at whose head he now so clearly stands.

Dow places the invention of this design "in the middle of the third century." *S.* xxi 360, however, which has been restored by Meritt to contain the "perfect design," is dated by him "*in. s.* iii:"

[- - - - - - - - - τ]ῶν π[ροέδρων] — stoichedon 28
[ἐπεψήφιζεν . . . 7 . . .]ίας Κ. . . 7 . . .
[. . . . . 12 . . . . . καὶ σ]υμπρόε[δροι· *vv*]
[*vvvvv* ἔδοξεν τεῖ βο]υλεῖ· *vvv* [*vvvvv*]
. . . . 15 . . . . ου Πιθεὺς ε[ἶπεν]·

Meritt's placing of the fragment at the beginning of the third century is supported by the lettering, but there are reasons, quite apart from the centring of the enactment formula, for favouring a much later date. In particular, Woodhead[63] points out that the formula employed in vv. 6-7 ([ἐπειδὴ . . . . 8 . . . .] βουλεύειν λ[αχὼν] | [ἐπὶ . . . 7 . . . ἄρχο]ντος) is not found before 256/5. Any of the archons of the years 291/0 (Charinos), 288/7 (Kimon), 280/79 (Gorgias), 254/3 (Philinos) and 253/2 (. . .bios) would fit the lacuna in v. 7; in order, however, to bring the document as close as possible to the middle of the century, we should perhaps allocate our text to one of the two possible years in the 250s.[64]

---

[61] *Art. cit.* (note 55) p. 64.

[62] Or in a line in which (in the interests of economy of stone) there are a very few letters spilled over from the previous line.

[63] See *Agora xvi* (forthcoming).

[64] Note that in a document of 318/17, *H.* xliii 1974, p. 464, Meritt intro-

duces isolation of the enactment formula in a line of 87 letters which is largely restored:

Γλαύκιππος Δεκελεεὺς [καὶ συμπρόεδροι· *v* ἔδοξεν τῶι δήμωι· *v* . . . . . .[27]. . . . . .
. . . . εἶπεν· ἐπειδὴ]

His purpose is to produce a space of exactly 27 letters in order to identify the orator with the purported orator of *S.* xxi 318. It is noticeable too that Meritt has also been obliged to introduce three uninscribed spaces at the end of the previous line. All in all, the restoration is open to doubt, but, if correct, will be our earliest example of an enactment formula set off by uninscribed space on either side.

CHAPTER FIVE

TO THE END OF THE THIRD CENTURY [1]

A. *Uninscribed spaces*

At the end of the last chapter we examined the use of uninscribed spaces to produce points of emphasis in the design of the prescript. In his discussion of the phenomenon [2] Dow offered a "table to show the designs of all dated preambles, 301/0-231/0," well aware, of course, that future discoveries could, and would, alter the chronology of the third century. He did not feel, however, that the reallocation of archons to new years would materially affect his results, and in this he was substantially correct. However, since the time he wrote there has also been a great increase in the number of dated texts available for study, and this, plus the necessary readjustments of the archon list, makes an up-to-date presentation of the evidence highly desirable. I therefore present the following table (pp. 68-69)—in somewhat greater detail than Dow's—in an attempt to give an overall picture of the means by which the enactment formula slowly and steadily moved towards the position of emphasis which it finally achieved in the 'perfect design.' [3] It can be seen that the earliest surely dated example of the 'perfect design' is ii²778, 250/49. This pushes down by a few years the terminus established by Dow.

Uninscribed spaces are also found before other items of the prescript, also for the purpose of emphasis.[4] The phenomenon occurs before the prytanising tribe,[5] the secretary item,[6] the lunar date,[7] the prytany date,[8] the meeting formula,[9] the name of the

---

[1] Some 120 texts form the basis of study for this chapter.

[2] *AJA* xl 1936, 66.

[3] [= as restored]; * denotes that other items in the same prescript are also set off by uninscribed spaces; EF = enactment formula.

[4] Or perhaps in some cases more punctuation rather than emphasis.

[5] ii²769, 233/2.

[6] ii²778, 259/49; ii²781, 250/49; ii²680, 249/8.

[7] ii²791, 247/6; ii²799 (*S.* xxi 391), 245/4; *H.* xvii 3-13, 3, 244/3; ii²798, 232/1.

[8] ii²770, 260/59.

[9] ii²778, 250/49; ii²799 (*S.* xxi 391), 245/4.

Methods of emphasising the enactment formula (to the end of the third century)

EF preceded by *vacat*(*s*) [10]	EF followed by *vacat*(*s*) [11]	*Vacat*(*s*) before and after EF, but EF not in a new line [12]	EF at beginning of new line in non-stoichedon text	EF at beginning of new line in non-stoichedon text, and followed by *vacat*(*s*) [13]	EF centred in a line vacant except for a few letters at the beginning—the "economy design"	EF centred [14] in a new line by itself—the "perfect design"
ii^{2}486, 304/3						
ii^{2}493, 303/2						
[*H*. ix 84-5.15, 283/2]						
S. xxv 89, 282/1						
	Ag.xv 76, 279/8		ii^{2}674 (Ag.xv 78), 273/2			
		ii^{2}772 (Sok. [1969] 40), 268/7 [15]				
		ii^{2}661, 267/6				
		[Ag.xv 81, 267/6]				
ii^{2}665, 266/5				ii^{2}666, 266/5		
[*S*. xxv 98, 265/4]		ii^{2}687, 265/4				
					ii^{2}702, (Ag.xv 87), 256/5	[*S*. xxi 360, ?254/3 or 253/2]
	Ag.xv 89, 254/3					
S. xxv 102, *c.m.s.* iii		*ii^{2}780 I, 252/1			[ii^{2}796, *m. s.* iii]	*ii^{2}778, 250/49
	*ii^{2}780 II 250/49					
						[*]ii^{2}781, 250/49
		*ii^{2}680, 249/8			ii^{2}683, 248/7	*H*. vii 121-3. 24, 249/8
					[*S*. xxiii 67, 246/5]	[*]ii^{2}679, 249/8
			[*ii^{2}799, 245/4]		**H*. xvii 3-13. 3, 244/3	*ii^{2}791, 247/6
					PM p. 25, 244/3	ii^{2}766 (*S*. xxi 392), 244/3
		ii^{2}784, 240/39				
						[*S*. xix 78, 239/8]

			ii^{2}787, 230/5
		*ii^{2}790 (Ag.xv 115), 235/4	ii^{2}788, 235/4
	*ii^{2}769, 233/2		
			ii^{2}833, 229/8
Ag.xv 120, 228/7			[*ii^{2}852 (*S.* xxi 396), b. 229/8 and 225/4]
			ii^{2}837, 227/6
			S. xxv 106, 226/5
			ii^{2}917 (Ag.xv 128), 223/2
			[ii^{2}848 I (Ag.xv 129), 222/1]
			ibid. II, 222/1
			ii^{2}839, 221/0
	ii^{2}843, 218/17		
ii^{2}794, 216/15			
		[ii^{2}912 I and II (Ag. xv 138), *c.* 210/09-201/200]	ii^{2}847, 215/14
[*H.* xlv 297-9 204/3]	Ag.xv 147 II, 203/2		
			[ii^{2}861 (*S.* xxi 406), *ante fin. s.* iii]
			[ii^{2}865, *fin. s.* iii]
			[Ag.xv 144, *fin. s.* iii]

---

[10] Some texts break off before it can be determined whether or not there are uninscribed spaces *after* the enactment formula.

[11] A *vacat* thus placed (between the enactment formula and the orator) may equally well be taken to be emphasising the *orator* (especially where it can be shown that a *vacat* did not also *precede* the enactment formula).

[12] The second *vacat* may, of course, be setting off the *orator*.

[13] ii^{2}660 II, 281/0, is a stoichedon text: hence the position of the enactment formula at the beginning of v. 29 is (largely) fortuitous.

[14] 'Centred' does not necessarily imply a precisely symmetrical position. Sometimes the 'centring' is slightly lopsided.

[15] The *vacat* in v. 8 has fallen out of Sokolowski's text.

chairman,[16] and of the orator.[17] It is also found with lists of names of symproedroi,[18] and before the minute-headings βουλῆς ψηφίσματα [19] and δήμου ψήφισμα.[20] Outwith the prescript itself it is also common before ἐπειδή [21] and between ἐπειδή and the name of the honorand.[22] It is noteworthy that, without exception, in any prescript which employs the device of uninscribed spaces, more than one item is always so set off.

B. *Other details*

(1) Superscripts: These continue to become more and more uncommon, and such examples as we do find occur exclusively in the first half of the century. θεοί, of course, is frequently inscribed, and on one occasion we find in its stead Μοῦσ[αι] on a stone honouring an agonothete for his conduct of, *inter alia*, the Dionysiac contests.[23] In a few instances the honorand appears superscript, in the nominative,[24] and in the genitive.[25] Two other examples of more elaborate formulations have special justification: in a document authorizing contributions by the Athenians towards the national defence and publishing lists of those who have so contributed, the Treasurer of the Military Fund is singled out for special prominence at the top of the stone: [26]

Ταμίας στρατιω[τικῶν]
Εὐρυκλείδης Μικίωνος [Κηφισιεύς]

and on the stone recording the granting of a request by the priest of the Hero Doctor to make a new oinochoe from the old dedications in the shrine we find at the head a dedicatory formula by one

---

16 I.e. immediately after the verb ἐπεψήφιζεν: ii²777, 252/1; ii²778, 250/49; ii²780 II, 250/49; ii²683, 248/7; ii²790 (Ag.xv 115), 235/4; ii²769, 233/2. Uninscribed spaces are found on *both* sides of the chairman's name in ii²780 I, 252/1.

17 ii²780 II, 250/49; ii²832, 229/8; Ag.xv 130 I, 220/19.

18 ii²770, 260/59; ii²700, 258/7; ii²832, 229/8; ii²852 (*S*. xxi 396), 229/8-225/4.

19 Ag.xv 130 I, 220/19.

20 ii²857, *ante* 224/3.

21 E.g. ii²680, 249/8; *H*. xlv 297-9, 204/3.

22 E.g. ii²784, 240/39; cf. ii²788, 235/4, where the double *vacat* at the end of v. 8 allows the name to stand at the very beginning of v. 9.

23 ii²780, 252/1.

24 ii²650, 286/5; ii²673, 278/7.

25 ii²651, 286/5; ii²658, 283/2; ii²703, *ante med.s*. iii.

26 ii²791, 247/6 (see *H*. xi 287-92.56).

Eukles, son of Eunomos of Kephale, who is mentioned at v. 79 of the text as one of the donors.[27] It is fairly clear that Eukles took it upon himself to set up this stone at his own private expense, and not unnaturally therefore commemorated his gesture by prefixing his name:

Ἥρωι ἰατρῶι
Εὐκλῆς Εὐνόμου
Κεφαλῆθεν
ἀνέθηκεν.
vacat
Θ ε ο [ί]

(2) Archon: The customary formula ἐπὶ τοῦ δεῖνος ἄρχοντος shows one or two variations. Particularly noteworthy are two texts where the formula becomes ἄρχων + nomen.[28] Why the secretary should have chosen to experiment with the now virtually immutable formulation is not at all clear: all that we can say is that this attempt to produce an alternative formulation did not succeed.

In two texts of the year 266/5 [29] the archon Nikias is given his demotic, in the sequence ἐπὶ Νικίου ἄρχοντος Ὀτρυνέως, no doubt to distinguish him from the homonymous holders of the office in 296/5 and 282/1. Nikias, of course, was an exceedingly common Athenian name.[30]

(3) Secretary: The secretary formula is not infrequently omitted.[31] In two instances of the same year (265/4),[32] although the secretary is not inscribed, a large *vacat* has been left on the stone sufficient to accommodate the formula. The only feasible explanation is that even by the fourteenth day of the third prytany the secretary of this year was still not known. Possibly the holder

---

[27] ii²839, 221/0.

[28] ii²658, 283/2 and *S.* xxv 90, 281/0, quoted above, in connection with the anagrapheis, on p. 55.

[29] ii²665 and 666.

[30] For ἄρχοντος omitted in the formula see ii²844 II, 222/1 (inscribed 193/2), p. 76 below.

[31] ii²705, *in.s.* iii; ii²662 *c.* Add. (*S.* xvi 62), 286/5; ii²655, 285/4 (but contrast ii²654 of the same day); *S.* xxi 370, 271/0 (but contrast other texts of the same year: *S.* xiv 64 and 65; Ag.xv 80); ii²850, 202/1.

[32] ii²687 (treaty with Sparta) and *S.* xxv 98, of prytanies II and III respectively.

had died in office and a successor had not yet been chosen.[33]

(4) Dating formulae: In 6 instances the prytany date is omitted,[34] and in one there is neither lunar nor prytany date.[35]

(5) Ecclesia formula: In two instances we have meetings of the ecclesia qualified by the phrase κατὰ ψήφισμα ὃ ND εἶπεν.[36] Presumably the additional qualification is meant to emphasise the fact that these were extraordinary meetings of the ecclesia for special purposes.

(6) Chairman: This item is omitted in four texts.[37] In one instance[38] only the words τῶ]ν προέδρων ἐπεψή|[φ]ιζεν have been inscribed, but a large *vacat* then follows with space enough to accommodate the name of the chairman and καὶ συμπρόεδροι.[39] It is noticeable that all[40] of these texts exhibit other peculiarities as well.

(7) Enactment formula and minute-headings: The enactment formula is lacking on some 7 occasions:[41] however, in four of these texts[42] appears a minute-heading, an item which first occurs late in the century. The earliest example, in the common, but illogical, *plural* form,[43] δήμου ψηφίσματα, is in ii²832, 229/8, where the item

---

[33] For a similar intentional leaving of uninscribed space to be filled in later cf. the Hekatompedon inventory of 411/10 (i²271 vv. 146-150) and the Pronaos inventory of the same year (i²247 vv. 192-195). The treasurers of 411/10 had their annual inventories inscribed before their successors had chosen a secretary. Although they left room on the stelai for his name, it was not subsequently filled in (see Wesley E. Thompson, *H.* xxxiv 1965, 305-6; id. *AJP* lxxxvi 1965, 169-170). Cf. also the *vacat* in the chairman-formula in ii²662 *c.* Add. (*S.* xvi 62), 286/5: see (6) above (with note 39).

[34] ii²659 (Sokolowski [1969] 39), 283/2; ii²674 (Ag.xv 78), 273/2; ii²772 (Sokolowski [1969] 40), 268/7; ii²661, 267/6; ii²477, 255/4; ii²798, 232/1; ii²850, 202/1.

[35] *S.* xxiii 67, 246/5.

[36] ii²838, 226/5; ii²857, *ante* 224/3. Cf. above p. 56.

[37] ii²659 (Sokolowski [1969] 39), 283/2; ii²680, 249/8; Ag.xv 130 I and II, 220/19.

[38] ii²662 *c.* Add. (*S.* xvi 62), 286/5.

[39] See Dow, *H.* xxxii 1963, p. 340. And cf. (3) above (with note 33).

[40] Except ii²680.

[41] ii²659 (Sokolowski [1969] 39), 283/2; ii²700, 258/7; ii²832, 229/8; Ag.xv 130 I and II, 220/19; Ag.xv 135, 214/13; ii²850, 202/1.

[42] ii²832, Ag.xv 130 I and II, Ag.xv 135.

[43] See Koehler on ii²839: "scriba aut lapicida δήμου ψηφίσματα parum adcurate posuit pro δήμου ψήφισμα."

appears immediately after the secretary and no enactment formula is expressed:

non-stoichedon

'Επὶ 'Ηλιοδώρου ἄρχοντος, ἐπὶ τῆς Πανδιονίδος ὀγδό
ης [πρ]υτανείας, ἧι Χαρίας Καλλίου 'Αθμονε[ὺ]ς ἐγραμ
[μάτε]υεν· δήμου ψ[η]φίσματα· 'Ανθεστηριῶνος κτλ.

It is found, similarly situated, in ii^{2}839, 221/0 (together with the enactment formula, albeit the wrong one),[44] and is restored in ii^{2}861 (*S.* xxi 406), *ante fin. s.* iii (with a totally restored enactment formula). In Ag.xv 135, 214/13, the phrase is found in the reverse order, [ψη]φίσματα δήμου (without enactment formula).

The singular form, δήμου ψήφισμα, is first found (restored), again immediately after the secretary, in ii^{2}849, 207/6 [45] and in ii^{2}857, *ante* 224/3 (with the enactment formula), and appears (unrestored) between ἐκκλησία κυρία and the orator [46] in Ag.xv 130 II, 220/19 (without enactment formula). This last text is seriously at fault: it is a decree of the boule, yet it is attributed to the demos both by ἐκκλησία κυρία and the minute heading.[47]

The equivalent minute-heading for decrees of the boule is first found, in the plural form βουλῆς ψηφίσματα, in Ag.xv 130 I.[48] Again it is incorrectly applied, for this is a decree of the demos. In this instance the heading appears between the prytany date and the orator, set off by single uninscribed spaces on either side. It is also found, immediately following the secretary, in ii^{2}847, 215/14 [49] and ii^{2}783, between 224 and 201.[50]

Texts with minute-headings occur sporadically down to the end of the first century. It seems, however, as if this feature was not entirely a success: indeed in many cases it appears to have created unnecessary confusion rather than further enlightenment.

---

[44] In v. 14 we read ἔδοξεν τεῖ βουλ[εῖ]: see Rhodes, *The Athenian Boule*, p. 77.

[45] The text breaks off before we can judge whether it included the enactment formula or not.

[46] The chairman is omitted.

[47] V. 39 is also in error: read πέμπτης for ἕκτης; see *H.* xxxviii 1969, 427-8.

[48] Again the enactment formula and the chairman are both omitted.

[49] Again carelessly applied: the enactment formula here shows that this was a probouleumatic decree.

[50] In this text the correct enactment formula is included.

(8) Orator: The orator appears to be lacking his patronymic in ii^{2}662 *c.* Add. (*S.* xvi 62), 286/5: [51]

stoichedon 43

ἔδοξεν τῆ

[ι βο]υλῆι καὶ τῶι δήμωι· . . . . .^{12}. . . . . Ἀφιδναῖος *v*
[εἶπεν·

A short *nomen* and *patronymicum* could, however, fit into the 12 available spaces and, in view of the otherwise ubiquitous patronymic, it is best not to assume that it is missing here.[52]

C. *Unusual prescripts*

(1) ii^{2}656 (*c.* Add. p. 662; Ag.xv 69), 284/3:

[θ] ε ο [ί].

non-stoichedon *c.* 30-35

Ἐπὶ Ἰσαίου· Ἐλαφηβολιῶνος πέμπτει ἱστα
μένου· Νικοκράτης Ἀρχεμάχου Φηγαιεύ[ς]
εἶπεν·

It seems certain that this is *not* a decree of the demos but a tribal decree of Aegeis.[53] We should read therefore in v. 10 δεδόχ[θ]αι [τεῖ φυλεῖ *aut* Αἰγεῖδαις].

Dow [54] confirms our suspicions by showing that the script and non-stoichedon arrangement of the text differ from the work of masons employed on public documents of this period and that the stele is smaller than any known public inscription in honour of prytaneis.

(2) ii^{2}659 (Sokolowski [1969] 39), 283/2: [55]

Ἐπὶ ἱερείας Ἡγησιπύλης. non-stoichedon
ἐπ' Εὐθίου ἄρχοντος, κτλ.

We have already commented on the lack of prytany date, chairman

---

[51] A text on which I have already commented with regard to the omission of the secretary (p. 71) and the leaving of a large *vacat* for the name of the epistates καὶ συμπρόεδροι. (p. 72).

[52] Note that in ii^{2}848 II (Ag.xv 129), 222/1, the orator's demotic is *not* omitted in v. 42. Θριάσιος is quite plainly read on the stone.

[53] So Wilhelm, *Ath. Mitt.* xxxix 1914, pp. 177 ff.

[54] *H.* Suppl. I, p. 36.

[55] Wrongly dated by Sokolowski.

and enactment formula in this decree on the sanctuary of Aphrodite Pandemos. The presence of the priestess in the prescript will recall ii²354, 328/7, the text in honour of the priest Androkles, in which the honorand was included (syntactically) with the archon.[56]

(3) *S.* xxi 371, 254/3:

['Επ]ὶ Φιλίνου ἄρχοντος, ---------- non-stoichedon
[. . . εἶ]πεν·

This small fragment offers no more than the archon and the orator. Conceivably it is a prescript of the extremely abbreviated form that we have noted in ii²457 and 463, both of the year 307/6.[57] Equally well, however, this may not be a decree of the state: it may well be a document of some lesser body.[58]

(4) ii²917 (Ag.xv 128), 223/2: The prescript to the 'second' text of this prytany decree reads simply:

non-stoichedon *c.* 48

Ποσιδεῶνος δευτέ[ραι ἱσταμένου,] δευτέρ[αι τῆς πρυτανείας·]
βουλὴ ἐν βουλευτη[ρίωι· τῶν προέδρ[ων ἐπεψ[ήφιζεν ------]
Φανοστράτου Φηγ[αιεὺς καὶ συμπ]ρόεδρο[ι· ἔδοξεν τῆι βουλῆι·]
'Αρκεσίλας Σωστρ[άτου . . . c. 8 . . . ε]ἶπεν·

This sort of curtailment of the prescript is not uncommon in the boule resolution following upon the resolution of the demos in prytany decrees, and probably also accounts for Ag.xv 144, *fin. s.* iii:[59]

non-stoichedon *c.* 36

[ἐπὶ τῆς ---------τρίτης καὶ δ]εκάτης πρυ
[τανείας· Σκιροφοριῶνος -----η]ι ἱσταμένου,
[----ηι τῆς πρυτανείας· βουλὴ ἐμ βο]υλευτηρίωι·
[τῶν προέδρων ἐπεψήφιζεν ------]δοτος Διο *v*.
[-------- καὶ συμπρόεδροι]· *vacat*
[ἔδοξεν τῆι βουλῆι]· *vacat*
[-------------------------εἶ]πεν·

---

[56] See p. 47 above.
[57] See pp. 61-62 above.
[58] Woodhead (Ag. xvi forthcoming) comes to the same conclusion, comparing ii²1270, 1287 and 1301.
[59] Meritt (*H.* xxxii 1963, p. 14) points out that this text does not come from the upper part of its stele: there is considerable uninscribed space above v. 1.

Cf. also Ag.xv 89, 254/3, v. 23, where the boule resolution is introduced by nothing more than the enactment formula and the orator:

Ἔδοξεν τεῖ βουλεῖ· Λυκομήδης Διοχάρου Κον[θ]υλῆ[θε]ν εἶπεν·

Cf. also ii^{2}678 (Ag.xv 85), 256/5, vv. 10ff.

ἐπὶ τῆς δω[δεκ]άτης πρυτανείας· [Σῖ?]μος Ἐπικράτου Αἰθαλίδης εἶ[π]ε[ν·

This example is somewhat different: for here, *after* the Council resolution, we have a further special decree in honour of Nikokrates, the Treasurer of both the prytaneis of Oineis and of the Boule. This third resolution is introduced merely by the number of the prytany and the orator.

(5) ii^{2}844 I, 229/8; II, 222/1; III, 193/2:

I. Θ ε ο ί.

non-stoichedon

Ἐπὶ Ἡλιοδώρου ἄρχοντος ἐπὶ τῆς Κεκροπίδος ἐνδεκά
της πρυτανείας· Θαργηλιῶνος· Λυσίστρατος Φυλαρχί
δου Οἰναῖος εἶπεν·

II. Ἐπὶ Ἀρχελάου· Ἀνθεστηριῶνος ἐμβολίμου· Διονύσιος Θεο
φίλου Ἐλαιούσιος εἶπεν·

III. Ἐπὶ Φαναρχίδου ἄρχοντος ἐπὶ τῆς Πανδιονίδος τρίτης
πρυτανείας· Βοηδρομιῶνος· Νικίας Πολ[υξ]ένου Πόριος εἶπε[ν]·

We have here three decrees all inscribed by the same hand in 193/2. Decree I and decree II are in honour of Eumaridas of Kydonia; decree III in honour of his son Charmion. All three have in common a considerably abbreviated form of prescript,[60] but it is not immediately clear why this should be so.

From decree II we may perhaps infer that decree I was never acted upon and never published.[61] It may be then that these three texts were put up privately by Charmion, at his own expense. If so, they are unofficial copies, based on information drawn from the state archives.

(6) ii^{2}850, 202/1, an award of citizenship to Alexander, son of Kallistratos of Thessaly:

[60] I and III are identical in form: II omits mention of the tribe in prytany (and, incidentally, omits the word ἄρχοντος in the archon item).

[61] Although the publication formula appears in vv. 28-30.

non-stoichedon *c*. 26-33

'Επὶ Διονυσίου ἄρχ[οντ]ος· 'Ελαφηβολι
ῶνος δευτέραι μετ' εἰκάδας· ἐκκλησί[α]
ἐμ Πειραιεῖ· Νικί[ας] Πολυξένου Πόριος
εἶπεν·

As in the case of the three prescripts of ii^{2}844, so too here we find a very abbreviated prescript to a decree in honour of a foreigner. The possibility therefore suggests itself (as an alternative to the erection of the stone by Alexander *suis impensis*) that at this period certain types of documents (e.g. honorary decrees for foreigners) were no longer felt to demand complete prescripts.[62]

Finally, as an example of a prescript containing all the canonical elements available at this time, consider, for the purposes of comparison, ii^{2}847, 215/14: [63]

'Επὶ Διοκλέους ἄρχοντο<ς> ἐπὶ τῆς 'Ιπποθωντί non-stoichedon
δος τρίτης καὶ δεκάτης πρυτανείας ἧι
'Αριστοφάνης Στρατοκλέους Κειριάδης ἐ
γραμμάτευεν· βουλῆς ψηφίσματα· Σκιροφο
ριῶνος τρίτει ἱσταμένου, τρίτει τῆς πρυτα
νείας· βουλὴ ἐμ βουλευτηρίωι· τῶν προέδρων [ἐ]
πεψήφιζεν Φανοκλῆς 'Ιππομάχου 'Αγγελῆθεν
καὶ συμπρόεδροι·
ἔδοξεν τεῖ βουλεῖ καὶ τῶι δήμωι·
Δημοκράτης Σουνιέως Κολωνῆθεν εἶπεν·

---

[62] For other examples which may admit of the same explanation, see below pp. 89-90.

[63] This is a probouleutic decree in which the minute-heading and the record of the place of meeting have been carelessly applied: see Rhodes, *op. cit.*, p. 77.

CHAPTER SIX

THE SECOND CENTURY AND ON TO THE CONQUEST OF ATHENS BY SULLA (86 B.C.) [1]

A. *Innovations*

(1) 'Triple dating': The most striking new development in the prescript of this period is the appearance in some documents of the so-called 'triple-dating' formula, 'triple' in the sense that the lunar section of the normal date by month and by prytany is given according to a double reckoning, κατ' ἄρχοντα and κατὰ θεόν. It is quite clear from the preserved equations that, whenever we have such a distinction in the civil date, the prytany date always corresponds to the date κατὰ θεόν.

Meritt had proposed [2] that the dates κατὰ θεόν were in fact dates according to Meton's astronomical calendar, but because of certain difficulties in this hypothesis his most recent view [3] is that the phrase κατὰ θεόν denotes " 'normal' or 'non-tampered,' in contradistinction to a date which has been irregularly advanced or retarded," added as a correction to clarify the situation when the real date had been 'adjusted' by the archon.[4]

All known dates κατὰ θεόν occur in the period 196/5 to 95/4. Previous writers on the phenomenon, concerned mainly with establishing calendar equations, have attempted to tabulate the evidence.[5] I construct below a table designed to indicate the precise *form* in which the three systems of reckoning were recorded:

One or two observations can immediately be made:

(i) nn. 2, 4 and 5 are triple dates only by implication. They all

---

[1] There are approximately 150 relevant texts for this period.

[2] *TAPA* xcv 1964, pp. 236 ff.

[3] In collaboration with John S. Traill, *The Athenian Agora*, Vol. xv, Inscriptions: *The Athenian Councillors*, 1974, pp. 23-4.

[4] In the year of Achaios (166/5), for example, the prytany date (at least from Anthesterion) was equated with a κατὰ θεόν date in which the months were one month ahead of the calendar date κατ' ἄρχοντα.

[5] Known examples were cited by Pritchett and Neugebauer, *Calendars*, p. 15. For variations see Meritt *TAY*, pp. 165-6; Pritchett, *Univ. of Cal. Pub. in Cl. Arch.* IV 4 1963, p. 336 n. 9 and p. 337; Meritt, *H.* xxxii 1963, 16-17, 15.

Evidence from decrees of boule and demos relative to triple dating [6]

	Date	Archon	Reference	Formulation	No. in *CPCA*
1.	196/5	Charikles	*S.* xxv 112 (*H.* v 419-28, 15)	MD, κατὰ θεὸν δὲ <date,> DP	4
2.	191/0	?	*S.* xxii 102 (*H.* v. 428-9, 16); Ἀρχ. Ἐφ. 1968, 96	MD κατὰ θε]όν, [DP]	18
3.	190/89	Demetrios	Ag.xv 171 (PM pp. 121-2)	MD, [κατὰ θεὸν δὲ] date, DP	5
4.	173/2	Alexis	*S.* xvi 92 (*H.* xvi 163, 61); Ἀρχ. Ἐφ. 1968, 96	[MD κατὰ θεόν, DP]	—
5.	173/2	Alexis	ii^{2}996 (*S.* xvi 93; *H.* xxvi 38-9); Ἀρχ. Ἐφ. 1968, 97	MD [κατὰ θεόν, DP]	—
6.	173/2	Alexis	Ag.xv 207 (*H.* xxxiii 183-4, 34); Ἀρχ. Ἐφ. 1968, 102	MD [κατ' ἄρχοντα, κατὰ θεὸν] δὲ date, DP	—
7.	166/5	Achaios	ii^{2}946; Ἀρχ. Ἐφ. 1968, 95	MD, [κατὰ θεὸν δὲ] date, [DP]	1
8.	166/5	Achaios	ii^{2}947; Ἀρχ. Ἐφ. 1968, 95-6	MD, [κατὰ θεὸν δὲ] date, DP	2
9.	164/3	Euergetes	Ag.xv 219 (*H.* xxvi 72-7, 22); Ἀρχ. Ἐφ. 1968, 103)	MD, κατὰ θεὸν δὲ date, DP	6
10.	161/0	Aristolas	*H.* xvi 164-8, 64	[MD, κατὰ] θεὸν δὲ date, D[P]	3
11.	155/4	Mnesitheos	ii^{2}979	[M]D, κατὰ [θεὸν δὲ] date, DP	9
12.	155/4	Mnesitheos	*H.* x 60-1, 25	[MD, κατὰ θεὸν δὲ date, D]P	10
13.	*med.s.* ii	?	ii^{2}1001	?[MD] κατ' ἄ[ρχοντα, κατὰ θεὸν δὲ date, DP]	19
14.	148/7 [7]	Lysiades	*S.* xxii 107 (*H.* xxxiv 89-90, 2)	MD [κατ' ἄρχοντα, κατὰ θεὸν δὲ] date, [DP]	—
15.	145/4	Metrophanes	ii^{2}967 (Ag.xv 238)	MD κατ' ἄρχοντα, κατὰ θεὸν δὲ date, DP	8
16.	127/6	Theodorides	*S.* xv 104 II	MD [κατ' ἄρχοντα, κατὰ] θεὸν [δὲ date], DP	17
17.	122/1	Nikodemos	ii^{2}1004 (Ag.xv 252)	MD [κατ' ἄρχοντα, κατὰ θεὸν δὲ date], D[P]	11
18.	122/1	Nikodemos	ii^{2}1006 I	MD κατ' ἄρχοντα, κατὰ θεὸν δὲ date, DP	12
19.	122/1	Nikodemos	*H.* x 61-2, 26	[MD, κατὰ θεὸν δὲ] date, [DP]	13
20.	95/4	Theodotos	Ag.xv 261 (*H.* xvii 25-9, 12) II	M[D κατὰ] θεόν, DP, κατ' ἄρχοντα [δὲ date]	15
21.	95/4	Theodotos	ibid. I	[MD] κατὰ θεόν, DP, [κατ' ἄρχοντα δὲ] date	16

[6] MD = month date; DP = date of prytany. (Note that Pritchett's n. 14 is deleted from the list: see *H.* xxxii 1963, 16-17, 15).

[7] Cf. also a decree of the Eumolpidai, of the same year: *S.* xix 124 (*H.* xi 293-8, 58): Π̣[υανοψ]ιῶνος ἕκ[τει ἐπὶ] | δέκα κατὰ θεόν, κατὰ δὲ ἄρ[χοντ]α πέμπτει [ἱστα]‖μένου (Pritchett's n. 7). There is, of course, no prytany date given in this document.

appear to be dates κατὰ θεόν equated with prytany dates, without any mention of κατ' ἄρχοντα dates whatsoever.

(ii) triple dating formulae are found from the year 196/5 on,[8] but, until the middle of the century, the phrase κατ' ἄρχοντα is not expressed on the stone. Nn. 13-21 show a quite consistent picture of full-blown triple dates.[9]

(iii) the only exception to (ii) is n. 6 (Ag.xv. 207), which appears to be the earliest example of κατ' ἄρχοντα by some 20 years. So unexpected is this occurrence that it leaves open to considerable doubt the allocation of this text to the year of Alexis.[10] In my opinion it would be much safer to assume on formal grounds that it belongs to a year in the second half of the century.[11] Apart from several 'blank' years where the secretaries are unknown, two years in particular could be considered likely candidates meeting all the requirements (intercalary; archon with name occupying *c.* 8 letter spaces; and a secretary with a demotic ending in -εύς): [12] 124/3, the year of the double archons [13] Nikias and Isigenes, where we could read either ἐπὶ 'Ισιγένου or ἐπ' 'Ισιγένους ἄρχοντος; and 119/18, the year of Hipparchos.

(iv) the last two examples (nn. 20, 21) display a new sequence, in which the 'real' lunar date and the prytany date both precede the 'tampered' archon date.

(2) The antigrapheus: A second innovation is the inclusion in the prescript of the ἀντιγραφεύς, an official who has not previously been mentioned in the recording of decrees. This official, who

[8] Although the example quoted from this year (*S.* xxv 112) is somewhat puzzling: κατὰ θεὸν δὲ was inscribed, but the date was never completed. The first true triple date is therefore Ag.xv 171 of the year 190/89.

[9] With the exception of the fragmentary n. 19 which appears to revert to the earlier formulation.

[10] It is perhaps significant that the *secretary* does *not* appear in any known inscription of the year of Alexis (see note 33 below).

[11] Pritchett refrains from arranging his list in chronological order, since, as he claims, "published lists of archons are too uncertain to permit assignment of many of these names." This is perhaps doing less than justice to Meritt's list in *TAY*, the allocations of which may be seen in some degree to be confirmed by the evidence presented in my table. (See now Meritt's latest list, *Historia* [forthcoming]).

[12] See *TAY*, p. 237.

[13] For years with double archons see E. A. Kapetanopoulos, *AAA* vii 3, 1974, 391-4 (summary p. 394).

presumably had secretarial duties of some kind,[14] makes his appearance in four documents of the second half of the second century. As in the case of the anagrapheus of the fourth and early third centuries the formula employed is ἀντιγραφεύς NPD; but unlike the anagrapheus, the antigrapheus does not seem to have attained any particular prominence. He is listed immediately after the secretary: e.g. ii²967 (Ag.xv. 238), 145/4:

non-stoichedon

['Επ]ὶ Μητροφάνου ἄρχοντος ἐπὶ τῆς 'Ακαμαντίδος δεκάτης πρυτα
νείας ἧι 'Επιγένης Μοσχίωνος Λαμπτρεὺς ἐγραμμάτευεν· ἀντι
γραφεὺς Δημοκράτης Δημοκράτου Κυδαθηναιεύς· 'Ελαφηβολιῶ-
νο[ς]
ἐνάτει μετ' εἰκάδας κατ' ἄρχοντα, κατὰ θεὸν [δ]ὲ Μουνιχιῶνος
δωδε[κά]
τει, δωδεκάτει τῆς πρυτανείας· ἐκκλησία κυρία ἐν τῶι θεάτρωι· τῶν
πρ[ο]
έδρων ἐπεψήφιζεν Τί[μυλλ]ος Τιμύλλου 'Ερχι[εὺ]ς καὶ συμπρόε-
δροι·
[ἔδοξ]εν τῶι δήμωι·
Τίμαρχος 'Επη[ρατίδ]ο[υ] Σφήττιος εἶπεν·[15]

Cf. Ag.xv 239, probably of the same prytany of the same year. Although this is a much more abbreviated prescript, the same antigrapheus, Demokrates son of Demokrates of Kydathenaion, is clearly read in vv. 3-4.

The third and fourth examples are somewhat different again. In *S.* xv 104 III and IV, 128/7, we find the antigrapheus cast in a longer formulation in which a clause is added naming the proposer of the decree which authorized the appointment of the antigrapheus to the staff of the Metroon:

III vv. 104-5:

non-stoichedon *c.* 82

ἀντιγραφεὺς 'Ηφαι[στ. . .c. 6. .]ΛΛ . . . . .c. 12. . . . .ι[ος
κατασταθεὶς ἐπὶ τὸ Μητρῶιον]
κατὰ τὸ ψήφισμα ὃ Τίμαρχος 'Επηρατίδου Σφ[ήττιος εἶπεν·

[14] For a discussion of this official about whom we know very little see Rhodes, *op. cit.*, pp. 238-9. His duties and status are far from certain. The comment in the *Corpus* (on ii²967) is not particularly illuminating: "scribae publico adlatus esse videtur, scilicet ut tabulas publicas contra signet."

[15] For the orator's patronymic see *H.* xv 1946, 212, note 25.

The formulation is identical in IV vv. 117-8.

(3) Uninscribed spaces: This feature, which we described in some detail in the last chapter, continues to develop, especially with regard to the enactment formula. The 'economy design' is found in some seven instances,[16] while the 'perfect design' occurs in at least 27 texts.[17]

It is noticeable that the orator's name is frequently preceded by uninscribed spaces, in particular in texts where the enactment formula does *not* occupy a separate line.[18]

B. *Other details*

(1) Superscripts: During the period under consideration, although θεοί continues to appear at the top of stones, there is not a single example of a superscript as such. The nearest we come to one is in ii²1009 (*H.* xvi 170-2, 67), 116/15, where, across the top of the stele in larger letters, we read:

Ἀγαθῆι [Τ]ύχηι.

This phrase had long been used to qualify the motion formula δεδόχθαι τῶι δήμωι, expressing the pious hope that good fortune would attend the motion under discussion. Now it appears in a more exalted position, but undoubtedly with the same implication.[19]

In two texts we find the phrase not superscript but as the first words of the prescript proper, immediately before the archon: e.g. ii²1011 I, 106/5:[20]

Ἀγαθῇ τύχῃ· Ἐπὶ Ἀγαθοκλέους ἄρχον[τ]ο[ς] κτλ.[21]

(2) Archon: We have commented above[22] on the addition of the demotic to the name of the archon Nikias (266/5) to distinguish him from other archons of the same name. We now find another

---

[16] E.g. ii²978 (*c.* Add. p. 670), 189/8; ii²1029, 96/5.

[17] E.g. *S.* xxv 112, 196/5; Ag.xv 261, 95/4.

[18] E.g. ii²916 (Ag.xv 187) II, 180/79; ii²1006 I, 122/1; ii²1008 II, 118/17; ii²1009 II, 116/15; ii²1028 I, 101/100.

[19] See P. Traywick, ΘΕΟΙ *and* ΑΓΑΘΗΙ ΤΥΧΗΙ *in Headings of Attic Inscriptions*, (unpublished dissertation), *HSCP* lxxiii 1969, 325-8.

[20] The fact that θεοί was also included superscript here shows that some distinction was felt between the two items.

[21] So also *ibid.* II, IV and V; and *S.* xxi 487, 99/8.

[22] P. 71.

device employed to meet the same need viz. the specifying of the archon as ὁ μετὰ τὸν δεῖνα: so Diodotos after Phanarchides,[23] possibly to avoid confusion with the Diodotos now placed in 205/4; [24] Philon after Menedemos; [25] Dionysios after Timarchides; [26] Dionysios after Lykiskos; [27] Dionysios after Paranomos,[28] and Jason after Polykleitos.[29] In each case the formula is ἐπὶ — ἄρχοντος τοῦ μετὰ —, the identifying phrase falling, like Nikias' demotic, *after* ἄρχοντος.[30]

In Ag.xv. 225 II, 155/4 we read:

non-stoichedon *c.* 44

'Επὶ Μν[ησ]ιθέου ἄρχο<ντος> ἐπὶ τῆς 'Ιπποθωντίδος δευτέρας πρυ

where ἄρχο could be regarded either as a deliberate abbreviation or as a careless mistake. Probably we should favour the latter assumption in view of the careless erasure at the end of v. 58 and the misspellings in vv. 114 and 121.[31]

A similar choice is open to us in *S.* xv 104 III, 128/7, where the stone reads:

'Επὶ Διονυσίου ἄρχοντος τοῦ με<τὰ> Λυκίσ[κον

and again one is inclined to set this down to the cutter's fault. In a text of this length, however, one should hardly be over-censorious at the odd mistake.[32]

(3) Secretary: In this period we find some 9 instances of omission of the secretary. It is noticeable that 4 of these occur in the same year, 173/2,[33] a fact which favours placing a fifth in that year

---

[23] ii²916 (Ag.xv 187) I (restored) and II, 192/1.

[24] See Traill, 'A Revision of *Hesperia* XLIII, 1974, "A New Ephebic Inscription from the Athenian Agora," *Hesperia* xlv 1976, 296-303.

[25] Ag.xv 194 I and II, 178/7. There is—as yet—no other nearby Philon as a candidate for contradistinction.

[26] Ag.xv 243 I and II, 135/4: probably to be distinguished from the archon Dionysios now restored in 141/0 (see Meritt, "Athenian Archons 347/6-48/7," *Historia* [forthcoming]).

[27] *S.* xv 104 III, 128/7, clearly distinguished from the homonym of 135/4.

[28] ii²1012, 112/111, clearly distinguished from the homonym of 128/7.

[29] ii²1014, 109/8, distinguished from Jason of 125/4.

[30] Cf. also ii²1056/7, *in.s.* i (?).

[31] See Dow, *Prytaneis* p. 153.

[32] See the *app. crit.* in *SEG*, which well indicates the slips this mason made.

[33] Ag.xv 206 I and II; *S.* xvi 92 and 93 (ii²996).

also.[34] Of the remaining 4 examples, one falls in the year 190/89,[35] where there are two other texts both containing the secretary; [36] a second in text II of a prytany inscription in which the secretary has already been named in text I; [37] the third, a somewhat curtailed prescript,[38] is a text of the same day as ii^{2}949, in which the secretary does appear; and the fourth is a fragmentary text of the year 94/3.[39]

The secretary is also omitted in three 'curtailed' prescripts.[40] The explanation of the omission may be either that the stones have been put up at private expense or simply that at this time less care was being given to express all the items of the prescript in their traditional form. In other words, we may have a reflection of the dwindling significance of, and lack of care and interest in, the resolutions of the Athenian body politic.

(4) Dating:

(i) Lunar date: This appears to be totally lacking in only one text.[41] In another we find the name of the month missing but the number of the day given.[42] A third anomaly is present in ii^{2}950 (*S.* xviii 22), 165/4, where the stone gives the name of the month (in the genitive) alone, followed by the prytany date: Σκιροφοριῶνος ἕκτει καὶ δ[ε]|κάτει τῆς πρυτανείας. This is emended in the *Corpus*, on the model of ii^{2}949, to read:

Σκιροφοριῶνος <ἕκτει ἐπὶ δέκα,> ἕκτει καὶ δ[ε]|κάτει τῆς πρυτανείας

assuming a haplography. But, in order to equate the 12 archon months of this year with the 13 conciliar months, Meritt [43] rejects

[34] *S.* xxi 452 (173/2-168/7, as dated in *SEG*). Both the historical circumstances and the space available for the archon's name would thus be satisfied. Stamires, however, opts for the vaguer parameters (*H.* xxvi 1957, 47-51).

[35] Ag.xv 171.

[36] Ag.xv 172 and *S.* xvi 76: see *TAY* pp. 184-7.

[37] Ag.xv 173 II, 189/8, one of the rare examples in prytany decrees where the decree passed by the Council was cut on the stone *above* the corresponding decree passed by the Demos. (Note too that in text II the prytanising tribe is also missing, again no doubt because it had already been specified in text I.)

[38] ii^{2}950 (*S.* xviii 22), 165/4: see 'Αρχ. 'Εφ. 1968, p. 100.

[39] ii^{2}1033 (*S.* xviii 29), a text which I discuss below (p. 93).

[40] ii^{2}954a (*H.* xli 46 II), ?166/5; ii^{2}971, 140/39; *S.* xxi 487, 99/8. (See also pp. 89-90 below).

[41] Ag.xv 202, 174/3.

[42] ii^{2}929, *c.in.s.* ii.

[43] *TAPA* xcv 1964, pp. 242-3; cf. 'Αρχ. 'Εφ. 1968, p. 100.

this equation and argues that the date ἕκτει ἐπὶ δέκα should in fact have been *omitted* in ii²949, just as it was in ii²950. He thus assumes a conflation arising from the prytany date in ii²949 rather than a haplography in ii²950.[44] If this is correct, we should emend the text of ii²949 to be in accord with ii²950, and so produce two examples of the month in the genitive without the day specified.[45]

(ii) Prytany date: In 3 clear instances [46] no prytany date appears, and in 4 others [47] the space available on the stone suggests that the item was also omitted there.

(5) Enacting body and place of meeting: I have already [48] discussed the inclusion of the words ἐκκλησία (κυρία) or βουλή, which appear regularly, but not invariably, from 336/5. From that time on we find — apart from the basic formulation—mention also of the *place* where the ecclesia was held e.g. ἐκκλησία ἐν Διονύσου; [49] ἐκκλησία (κυρία) ἐν τῶι θεάτρωι; [50] ἐκκλησία ἐμ Πειραιεῖ; [51] and also indications of meetings of the boule other than those held in the bouleuterion [52] e.g. βουλὴ ἐν τῶι Παναθηναϊκῶι σταδίωι; [53] βουλὴ ἐμ Πειραιεῖ,[54] and a meeting transferred from the bouleuterion to the Eleusinion: βουλὴ ἐν [βο]υ[λε]υτ[ηρίωι καὶ ἐκ] τοῦ βουλευτηρίου ἐν τῶι 'Ελευ|σινίωι.[55] We have also met examples of the more elaborate formulation which indicates that the meeting was held "in accordance with a decree of the people/boule" or "in accordance with a decree moved by —." [56]

---

[44] Meritt does, however, offer an alternative suggestion: the extra 30 days may have been absorbed during the first 6 prytanies of the year.

[45] Note also Ag.xv 239, 145/4, a text with an antigrapheus, where the month in the genitive (without the day) is restored to appear after a minute-heading which follows the antigrapheus.

[46] ii²897, 185/4; Ag.xv 239, 145/4; ii²971, 140/39.

[47] ii²898, 185/4 (possibly the same day as ii²897); *S.* xxi 452, 173/2-168/7 (?173/2); ii²954a (*H.* xli 46 II), ?166/5; ii²1056/7, *in.s.* i (?).

[48] See pp. 38-39 above (with note 31).

[49] E.g. ii²345, 332/1 etc. The regular meeting of the ecclesia following the Dionysia was held in the precinct of the god. This is to be distinguished from the frequent meetings ἐν τῶι θεάτρωι. See Busolt-Swoboda, *Griechische Staatskunde* II, 991 and note 2.

[50] E.g. ii²389 (*S.* xxi 354), 293/2; Ag.xv 120, 228/7.

[51] Ag.xv 165, 197/6.

[52] The normal meeting place.

[53] E.g. *H.* xlv 297-9, 204/3.

[54] ii²783, b. 224-201.

[55] ii²848 (Ag.xv 129) II, 222/1.

[56] See above p. 56 and p. 72.

When we now enter the second century we find a great deal more elaboration of detail [57] in these records of enacting bodies and their places of meeting. Of particular interest is a formulation used for meetings convened for the election of generals, found first in ii^{2}892, 188/7: vv. 5-6:

non-stoichedon *c.* 30-32

ἐκκλησία]
ἀρχαιρεσίαι κατὰ τὴν μαντ[είαν τοῦ θεοῦ.] [58]

and in ii^{2}954a (*H.* xli 46, II), vv. 2-4, in the longer form:

non-stoichedon *c.* 38

βουλὴ ἐμ] βουλευτηρίω̣[ι σύ]νκλητος στρατη
[γῶν παραγγειλά]ν̣των κ̣[α]ὶ ἀπ̣[ὸ βουλ]ῆς ἐκκλησία ἀρ
[χαιρεσίαι κατὰ τ]ὴν μαντ[είαν τοῦ] θεοῦ·

Meritt argued that all three texts (ii^{2}892, 954a and 955) belonged to the same day of 188/7. But Tracy [59] has now shown that the new join of ii^{2}954a and Ag. I 2105(*S.* xxv 124) leaves insufficient space to allow the restoration [ἐπὶ Συμμάχου ἄρχο]ν̣τος. He argues strongly for the year of Achaios (166/5), pointing out *inter alia* that, although ii^{2}954a is an extremely abbreviated prescript,[60] yet it includes the entire phrase βουλὴ ἐμ βουλευτηρίωι σύνκλητος στρατηγῶν παραγγειλάντων καὶ ἀπὸ βουλῆς ἐκκλησία κτλ., as if this phrase were an essential ingredient even when other items of the prescript could be omitted. Yet ii^{2}892, with a full prescript, does *not* include the whole phrase.[61] Tracy therefore concludes that this is strong supporting evidence that the two [62] decrees were not passed at the same session.

It should be stressed, however, that the year of Achaios is not the only suitable slot for ii^{2}954a + Ag. I 2105. Hippias, now

---

[57] Note ii^{2}1011 V, 107/6, where the theatre is rather superfluously described as being in the precinct of Dionysos: ἐκκλησία ἐν τῷ θεάτρωι ἐν Διονύσου.

[58] Also found (almost entirely restored) in ii^{2}955, dated on the same day as ii^{2}892 by Meritt, *Klio* lii 1970, 277-282.

[59] *H.* xli 1972, 46-9.

[60] See below pp. 89-90.

[61] Tracy's argument, however, against assuming a haplography such as ΕΠΙΣΥΜΜΑΡΧΟΝΤΟΣ is not valid: cf., e.g., Ag.xv 76, 279/8 where the stone reads [Ε]ΠΙΝΑΞΙΚΡΑ[ΤΟΥΣ for ἐπὶ Ἀναξικράτους (although the first iota may be in error for alpha and the text could read ἐπ' <Ἀ>ναξικράτους.

[62] Tracy rightly ignores the evidence (such as it is) of the fragmentary ii^{2}955.

restored to 181/0 since Tracy wrote, would be a possibility; and, as Woodhead points out,[63] so would Eunikos (169/8), if we elide the iota of ἐπί.[64] Whatever date, however, we assign to this text, it is clear that we now have evidence on stone for *two* occasions when a meeting of the assembly was held to elect the military officers.

A similar formula for a meeting of the boule followed by a meeting of the ecclesia is found in ii^{2}897, 185/4 vv. 4-6:

βουλὴ ἐμ βουλευτηρίωι σύνκλητος στρατ[ηγῶν]
παραγγειλάντων καὶ ἀπὸ βουλῆς ἐκκλησία [κυρία]
ἐν τῶι θεάτρωι·

as also in Ag.xv. 167, 181/0.[65]

Other formulae also appear recording the transference of a meeting from one venue to another: e.g. ii^{2}893a, 188/7 [66] vv. 5-7:

ἐ̣κ̣κ̣λη non-stoichedon
[σία ἀπὸ βουλῆς ἐν τῶι] θεάτρωι μεταχθε[ῖ]σα ἐκ *v*
[Παναθηναϊκοῦ σταδίο]υ·

cf. Ag.xv 177, a text of the same day, which has the further specification of the proposer of the resolution authorising the move: vv. 3-5:

non-stoichedon *c.* 54
βουλὴ ἐν τ[ῶι θε]
[άτρωι μεταχθεῖσα ἐκ Παναθηναϊκοῦ σταδί]ου κατὰ ψήφι[σμα τοῦ]
[δήμου δ --- *c.* 12 --- εἶπεν·

[63] Ag.xvi (forthcoming).

[64] Moreover, just as ii^{2}894 is *later* than the time of Attalos to whom the text refers, so too ii^{2}954a + Ag. I 2105 could be later than Eumenes (note πρότερον restored in v. 6): if so, then Pyrrhos (158/7) is yet another candidate for the archon of our text.

[65] *Pace* Tracy (*art. cit.*, p. 49, note 26), who claims that "the exact phrase is fully preserved only once elsewhere, in I.G., II^2, 897 (185/4)." It also seems to me to be going beyond the evidence to claim that "enough of the phrase is preserved in I.G., II^2, 898 to render it probable that the whole phrase occurred." (Tracy, *ibid.*, note 27).

[66] For the restoration of this text see Meritt, *Klio* lii 1970, 282, and now the commentary on Ag.xv 177 (p. 152), where Meritt reverts to a suggestion originally made in *AJPh* lxxviii 1957, 377 for the meeting formula.

Similarly, we find meetings of the ecclesia in the Theatre transferred from the Peiraeus, again with the further qualification κατὰ τὸ ψήφισμα ὃ — εἶπεν.[67]

(6) Chairman: This item is omitted in a few texts, especially texts which are otherwise also deficient.[68] In *S.* xxv 118, 169/8, the item is omitted but three lines are left almost entirely uninscribed, clearly to accommodate the formula at a later date: [69]

τῶν προέδρων ἐπεψήφι non-stoichedon *c.* 30
ζεν *vacat*
vacat
vacat

In one instance only the phrase καὶ συμπρόεδροι is missing, or apparently missing: *S.* xv 104 I, 127/6: [70]

non-stoichedon *c.* 53-74
τῶν προέδρων ἐπε
ψήφιζεν Ἀνδρόνικος [Ἀνδρονίκου Βουτάδης· ἔδοξεν τῶι δή-
μωι]· *vacat*
Πολύχαρμος Πολυκρ[ίτου Ἀζηνιεὺς εἶπεν·

It seems much more likely, however, that we should read in v. 4:

Ἀνδρόνικος [Ἀνδρονίκου Βουτάδης καὶ συμπρόεδροι]. *vacat*

a restoration which brings the text to exactly the same point before the *vacat.* The omitted item will then be, as not uncommonly, the enactment formula.[71]

(7) Enactment formula and minute-headings: The enactment formula is omitted on 8 occasions,[72] on one of which, however, we

---

[67] ii^{2}977 (Ag.xv 246), 131/0; *S.* xvi 102, *c.* 150-100; (?*S.* xvi 88, 176/5).

[68] *S.* xxi 452, 173/2-168/7 (?173/2); ii^{2}954a (*H.* xli 46 II), ?166/5; ii^{2}950 (*S.* xviii 22), 165/4; ii^{2}1027, *c.* 160; Ag.xv 239, 145/4; ii^{2}971, 140/39; *S.* xv 104 III, 128/7; *S.* xxi 490, *in.s.* i.

[69] See pp. 71-72 above (with notes 33 and 39).

[70] Contrast S. xv 104 II and IV (?)

[71] As in text III of this stone. Room for the enactment formula could, of course, be found in the *vacat*, making a total of 63 letters in v. 4. V. 5 has 64 letters.

[72] Ag.xv 171, 190/89; Ag.xv 172, 190/89; Ag.xv 173 I, 189/8; ii^{2}899 (Ag.xv 179), 185/4; *S.* xxi 452, 173/2-168/7 (?173/2); ii^{2}954a (*H.* xli 46 II), ?166/5; Ag.xv 239, 145/4; *S.* xv 104 III, 128/7. Probably also in ii^{2}1056/7, *in.s.* i (?).

find the minute-heading βουλῆς ψηφίσμ[ατα].[73] It is also excluded from the restored text of *H*. Suppl. iv, p. 145, 181/0, where Thompson inexplicably restores [βουλὴ ἐμ βουλευτηρίωι] precisely where one would expect the enactment formula to occur. This is surely an oversight and should be corrected to read [ἔδοξεν τεῖ βουλεῖ]. This will produce a line of 79 letters, as in v. 10 where the archon appears.

δήμου ψήφισμα(τα) occurs in a number of texts, always [74] after the secretary. It is frequently difficult to decide whether the singular or plural form should be restored, but it seems probable that the plural form was much the commoner.[75] It also appears that there is no text with δήμου ψήφισμα(τα) which does not also include the enactment formula.[76]

Likewise, with βουλῆς ψήφισμα(τα) it is not always clear whether to read singular or plural. However, there is no surely attested example of the singular, whereas the plural is read clearly in two instances.[77] The phrase seems normally to come immediately after the secretary, but in one instance it appears in the late position after the date by prytany.[78] The enactment formula would appear usually to be included, although we have one certain instance of its omission.[79]

C. *Curtailed prescripts*

There are 3 extremely curtailed prescripts:

(1) ii²954a (*H*. xli 46 II), ?166/5,[80] an honorary decree for Pausimachos:

non-stoichedon *c*. 38

['Επὶ 'Αχαίου ἄρχο]ντος· Μουνιχι[ῶνο]ς δευτέραι μετ' ε[ἰ]

---

[73] ii²899 (Ag.xv 179), 185/4.

[74] Except *S*. xvi 92 and ii²996 (*S*. xvi 93), of 173/2, in both of which the minute-heading appears after the prytanising tribe, but simply because the secretary item has been omitted.

[75] Definitely plural—ii²929, *c. in. s.* ii; *S*. xxv 112, 196/5; ii²1134 v. 65, 117/16; definitely singular—ii²890 (Ag.xv 174), 188/7.

[76] But many texts break off before the crucial point.

[77] *H*. Suppl. iv 144-7 (*S*. xxi 441), 181/0; Ag.xv 216, 166/5.

[78] *H*. Suppl. iv 144-7 (*S*. xxi 441), 181/0 (even although the secretary is included).

[79] ii²899 (Ag.xv 179), 185/4.

[80] I restore 'Αχαίου, as recommended by Tracy, *art. cit.* (but see above pp. 86-88), where we also discussed the meeting formula.

[κάδας· βουλὴ ἐμ] βουλευτηρίῳ[ι σύ]νκλητος στρατη
[γῶν παραγγειλά]ν̣των κ̣[α]ὶ ἀπ̣[ὸ βουλ]ῆς ἐκκλησία ἀρ
[χαιρεσίαι κατὰ τ]ὴν μαντ[είαν τοῦ] θεοῦ· Τίμων Α[.]
[. . . . . . c. 15 . . . . . .] Ṇ∆̣ [c. 3 εἶπεν·]

(2) ii²971, 140/39, an award of citizenship to Telesias of Troezen:

non-stoichedon 42-50

Ἐπὶ Ἁγνοθέου ἄρχοντος· Σκιροφοριῶνος ὀγδόει μετ' [εἰκάδας]·
ἐκκλησία ἐν Πειραιεῖ· ἔδοξεν τῆι βουλῆι καὶ τῶι δήμ[ωι]·
Καλλίμαχος Φαίδρου Ξυπεταιὼν εἶπεν·

(3) *S.* xxi 487, 99/8, a fragmentary decree: [81]

[Θ] ε [ο ί].

non-stoichedon *c.* 37

Ἀγαθῆ[ι τύ]χη[ι. ἐ]πὶ Πρ[οκλέους ἄρχοντος· Βοηδρο]
[μ]ιῶνο[ς ὀ]γδό[ηι μ]ετ' ε[ἰκάδας· βουλὴ ἐν τῶι Ἐλευ]
[σ]ινίωι· Ε. . Υ. Ν. . . ΛΑ ----------------------
. . ΟΙ ------------------------------------

These three texts seem to share certain features in common: complete absence of any reference to the prytanising tribe, the secretary, the prytany date and the chairman. No. 2 honours a foreigner, as does 1 also probably. One may perhaps assume that, with certain categories of documents (?honorary decrees for foreigners), it was no longer felt necessary at this period to inscribe prescripts with full details. The less likely alternative is to allocate these texts to private publication.[82]

D. *Unusual prescripts*

(1) Ag.xv 165, 197/6: in publishing this text Dow [83] assumed that an entire line had been accidentally omitted after v. 1. He therefore restored as follows:

non-stoichedon *c.* 40

Ἐπὶ Ἀγκύλου ἄρχοντος ἐπὶ τῆς Πανδιονίδος δεκ[ά]
<της πρυτανείας ἧι ---------- ἐγραμμάτευεν·
Μουνιχιῶνος(?) δεκά>
τει ὑστέραι, τετάρτει καὶ εἰκοστεῖ τῆς πρυτανε[ίας·

[81] The nature of this decree is uncertain.
[82] Cf. also ii²850, 202/1 (see pp. 76-77 above).
[83] *H.* Suppl. i, 86-8, 38.

Meritt,[84] however, denies the necessity to posit any such slip at all and reads:

> Ἐπὶ Ἀγκύλου ἄρχοντος ἐπὶ τῆς Πανδιονίδος· δεκ[ά]
> τει ὑστέραι, τετάρτει καὶ εἰκοστεῖ τῆς πρυτανε[ίας·

Neither the omission of the word πρυτανείας[85] in v. 1 nor of the name of the month will occasion us much surprise:[86] but the omission of the ordinal number of the prytanising tribe will certainly raise some doubt about the correctness of Meritt's suggestion. The parallel which he quotes[87] is hardly exact, since the ordinal omitted in i^{2}304B is not in a prescript at all.

(2) PM p. 120, 176/5:[88]

> c. 52
> Ἐπὶ Ἱππάκου ἄρχοντος ἐπὶ [τῆς . . . c. 9 . . . πρυτανείας ἧι Χαρῖνος]
> Σωκράτου Ἰφιστιάδης ἐγ[ραμμάτευεν· μηνὸς . . . . . . c. 18 . . . .]
> [. . .] ἐσιόντος, μιᾶι καὶ [τριακοστεῖ τῆς πρυτανείας· ἐκκλησία κυ-ρία]·
> [τῶ]ν προέδρων ἐπε[ψήφιζεν . . . . . . c. 15 . . . . . . καὶ συμπρόεδροι· ἔδοξεν]
> [τεῖ βουλεῖ] καὶ τῶι [δήμωι -]
> [- - - - - - - - - -]ι[- -]

Quite apart from the spatial difficulties mentioned in the footnote below we have here a quite unique formulation for the lunar date, if only in the use of ἐσιόντος for ἱσταμένου.[89]

PM claim that the unique phraseology is to be compared with ii^{2}951, 167/6, where we read:

> Ἐπὶ Νικοσθένου ἄρχον[τος, μηνὸς Ποσιδεῶνος]
> πέμπτει ἀπιόντος

---

[84] *TAY* pp. 170-2.

[85] Cf. e.g., ii^{2}218, 346/5; ii^{2}224, 343/2.

[86] Cf. e.g., ii^{2}500, 302/1.

[87] i^{2}304B (as in *Athenian Financial Documents* p. 120 v. 71).

[88] For the secretary's name and patronymic see Meritt, *H.* xxvi 1957, 69-71. With the restoration as made it seems inevitable that one must assume that some part of the prytanising tribe item has been omitted, whether the ordinal numeral (but Meritt should *not* quote *H.* iii 28, 20, 163/2 as a parallel for omission of the ordinal; see his own correction in *H.* xiii 1944, p. 266) or, more likely, the word πρυτανείας. (One might add that *c.* 15 spaces seem far too few for an epistates with name, patronymic and demotic). Altogether this is a puzzling stone.

[89] ἐσ- for εἰσ- is likewise remarkable in a text of this date.

but this is misleading. Had PM continued with the quotation of ii²951 it would have been apparent that it is not a prescript to a decree but a record of an oath sworn between the Athenians, Ambraciots and Acarnanians, which is dated according to the calendar systems of all three compacting parties. The form chosen to express the Athenian lunar date has been influenced by a desire to make the phraseology consistent with that employed for the other two parties. It is therefore in no way a parallel to the present document which remains unique and unexplained.[90]

(3) In 6 texts the 'prescript' consists of nothing more than the orator item. Two of these [91] have a superscript θεοί, removing any suspicion that the top of the stone may have been lost. The other four are all honours for the agonothetes of the Theseia.[92] Possibly again we have examples here of official 'pruning' [93] of the prescript. An alternative explanation of the latter four documents is that they all belonged to a single monument and that some superior stone carried the details absent from the individual texts.[94]

(4) ii²1014, 109/8: In this text (which goes no further than the enactment formula) a fairly lengthy item intervenes between the secretary and the lunar date:

non-stoichedon

Ἐπὶ Ἰάσονος ἄρχοντος τοῦ μετὰ Πολύκλει[τον ἐπὶ τῆς - - -ίδος τετάρτης πρυτανεί]
ας ἧ Ἐπιφάνης Ἐπιφάνου Λαμπτρεὺς ἐγρα[μμάτευεν· περὶ ἱερῶν· Καλλικρατίδης?]
Καλλικράτου Στειριεὺς γράμματα τάδε π[αρέδωκεν εἰς τὴν βουλὴν καὶ τὸν δῆ]
μον· *v* Πυανοψιῶνος ἕκτῃ ἱσταμένου, πέ[μπτηι τῆς πρυτανείας· βουλὴ ἐμ βουλευτη]

[90] Cf. however ii²1077 (Ag.xv 460), A.D. 209/10 v. 5: μηνὸς Ποσειδεῶνος τῇ ε̄ῑ.

[91] Honours for a merchant, ii²903, *c.* 176/5; and for a magistrate, *S.* xxv 126, 145/4.

[92] ii²956, 161/0; ii²957, 157/6; ii²959, *c.* 150; ii²958, 149/8.

[93] Such pruning unquestionably occurred in late prytany decrees: see below pp. 99-100.

[94] I owe this suggestion to Mr. A. G. Woodhead, who observes that the place of finding of all four is the same. See also E. Vanderpool, *H.* xliii 1974, 309.

ρίωι· τῶν προέδρων ἐπεψήφιζεν Δεξίχαρις Φι[. . . . . c. 13 . . . . .
ἀντιγραφεύς? Στρα?]
τιος Φηγαιεύς·
ἔδο[ξεν τῆι βουλῆι καὶ τῶι δήμωι·]

This is quite unparalleled elsewhere.

(5) ii^{2}1033 (*S.* xviii 29), 94/3: This extremely fragmentary prescript presents a unique mention of νουμηνία,[95] apparently in a formula of some length immediately after the prytany date and before the meeting record:

Θ [ε ο ί].
non-stoichedon 56-61
Ἐπὶ Καλ[λίου ἄρχοντος ἐπὶ τῆς - - - - ος - - - -ς πρυτανείας]·
Ἀνθεστη[ριῶνος . . . . c. 38 . . . . .ι τῆς]
πρυτανε[ίας . . . . c. 45 . . . .
. .]
νουμηνίαι ρ[. . . . . c. 42 . . . .
βου]
λὴ ἐν βουλε[υτηρίωι· τῶν προέδρων ἐπεψήφιζεν . . . . . . c. 19 . . . .
. . . . .]
Μυρρινούσ[ιος καὶ συμπρόεδροι· ἔδοξεν τῆι βουλῆι· . . . . c. 12 . . . .
ἐγ Μυρ]
ρινούττης [εἶπεν·

Whatever is to be restored in the lacuna in vv. 4-5, it seems certain that it is not part of the date of the decree, not because it is impossible to incorporate a triple-date in this text,[96] but because the space between πρυτανείας and νουμηνίαι is far too long for the κατ' ἄρχοντα δέ item. V. 5 of this prescript must remain a mystery until such time as some further fragment of this text is discovered.

The later the date, the more difficult it becomes to find a quotable prescript incorporating all the possible elements now available. ii^{2}967 (Ag.xv 238), 145/4 (already cited in full on p. 81) is a useful example from the middle of the century. For a later example,

[95] See Pritchett and Neugebauer, *Calendars* p. 31: "we have discovered no Athenian decree which is dated on the first day of any civil month."
[96] *Pace* Dinsmoor, *AA*, p. 414 with note 1. Nn. 20 and 21 (p. 79 above) show that a sequence month date κατὰ θεόν, date of prytany, κατ' ἄρχοντα δὲ date is more than likely at this date.

which does *not* include triple-dating or the antigrapheus, we might consider ii^{2}1028, I 101/100:

non-stoichedon 56-66

'Αγαθῆι τύχηι. 'Επὶ Μηδείου ἄρχοντος ἐπὶ τῆς Λεωντίδος τρίτης πρυτανείας ἧ Φιλί
ων Φιλίωνος 'Ελευσίνιος ἐγραμμάτευεν· Βοηδρομιῶνος ἐνάτηι ἱσταμένου, ἐνάτη
τῆς πρυτανείας· ἐκκλησία κυρία ἐν τῶι θεάτρωι· τῶν προέδρων ἐπεψήφιζεν 'Επιτέλης
'Αρεταίου Παιανιεὺς καὶ συμπρόεδροι· *vvvv* ἔδοξεν τῶι δήμωι· *vvvvv* Νικόστρατος
Δημαρέτου Λαμπτρεὺς εἶπεν·

CHAPTER SEVEN

AFTER SULLA [1]

A. *Innovations*

(1) Archaising prescripts: In two inscriptions, widely separated in time, we find a deliberate return to the old style prescript: ii²1071 (*S.* xvii 34), ?22/1, celebrating the birthday of Augustus. This is also noteworthy as the latest example of the stoichedon style from Athens: [2]

stoichedon 39

[Ἔδοξεν τῆι βουλῆι]· Αἰαντὶς ἐ[πρυτάνευε, . . .⁶. . . ἐ]
[γραμμάτευε, ...]ιος ἐπεστάτ[ει, ...⁹. . . . ἦρχε]·
[Ἀντίπατρος *vv*] Ἀντιπάτρου *vv* Φλ[υεὺς *vv* εἶπε· *vv*]

The sequence follows the traditional form, except that the orator, set out with distinguishing *vacats*, is assigned a patronymic and demotic.[3]

ii²1078 (Sokolowski [1969] 8), A.D. 221/2, the latest prescript available for this study. It is a decree outlining the functions of the ephebes in the Eleusinian festival: [4]

non-stoichedon

[Ἔδοξεν τ]ῶι δήμωι· Ἀραβιαν[ὸς ἦρχεν, ... ἐπρυ]
[τάνευε]ν, Εὔτυχος ἐγραμ[μάτευεν, ... ἐπε]
[στάτει· Δ]ρυαντιανὸς ἄρχων [τῶν Εὐμολπιδῶν εἶπεν]·

Apart from the elevation of the archon to second position, this text is very similar to ii²1071. The orator is without patronymic and demotic, but is given a qualifying phrase.[5]

---

[1] There are only some 27 texts available for study in this period. The latest, ii²1078, is dated A.D. 221/2.

[2] And, apart from an inscription from Oinoanda in Lykia, perhaps the latest stoichedon inscription from the whole of Greece: see R. P. Austin, *The Stoichedon Style in Greek Inscriptions*, London 1938, pp. 114 and 117-8.

[3] "It is not a survival of the stoichedon style but rather a revival with all the attendant formulae of decrees of the early fourth century before Christ" (Stamires, *H.* xxvi 1957, p. 262).

[4] It is perhaps significant that this is a religious text. The old style prescript may have been considered appropriately archaic.

[5] See below p. 99.

(2) The strategos epi ta hopla: [6] This official, new to the prescript, makes a prominent intrusion into ii²1039 (*S.* xxii 110), 79/8. He appears there both second to the archon and as the proposer of the decree:

Θ ε [ο ί]. non-stoichedon *c.* 65-75

['Επὶ . . . .]ου ἄρχοντος, στρατηγοῦντος ἐπὶ τοὺς ὁπλίτας Μνα-σ[έου τοῦ]
Μνασ[έου Βερ]ενικίδου· βουλῆς ψηφίσματα· Βοηδρομι[ῶ]νος ἕκτη ἱστα[μένου· ἐ]ν τῶι
Θησε[ίωι ἐκ] σταδ[ίου]· Μνασέας Μνασέου Βερεν[ικίδης] εἶπεν· [7]

Note the chiastic arrangement in v. 2.[8]

B. *Other details*

(1) Superscripts: θεοί appears for the last time in ii²1039 (*S.* xxii 110), 79/8.[9] Other superscripts are unknown,[10] except for ii²1043, ?37/6, where, above the decree, we read Σῶσις Σώσιδος 'Oῆθεν ὑπὲρ τῶν [συνεφήβω]ν ἀνέθηκεν. In this instance one of the ephebes, himself honoured in the fourth decree of the inscription,[11] has privately arranged for the publication of this lengthy ephebic monument.

The phrase ἀγαθῆι τύχηι τῆς βουλῆς καὶ τοῦ δήμου τοῦ 'Αθηναίων is found in three texts: Ag.xv 266, 64/3, where it occupies the whole of v. 1, thus allowing the archon to come right at the beginning of v. 2; and ii²1046 (Sokolowski [1969]44), 52/1 and ii²1043, ?37/6, where the phrase simply precedes the archon in the first line.[12]

Similarly in ii²1069 (+1119), *aet.imp.Aug.*, we find:

ἀγαθῆι τύχηι τοῦ Σεβαστοῦ Καίσαρος κ̣[- - - - - - - - - - - - ἐπὶ]
Λάκωνος ἄρχοντος, κτλ.

(2) Archon: The device of giving further qualification to the

[6] For this official see Daniel J. Geagan, *The Athenian Constitution after Sulla*, *H.* Suppl. xii 1967, 18-31.
[7] ii²1072, bet. A.D. 91/2 and 97/8 is another example of a decree moved by the strategos epi ta hopla: see Rhodes, *op. cit.*, pp. 46-7.
[8] Cf. p. 47 above (with note 73).
[9] Quoted above.
[10] I exclude the 'citations' which appear superscript in some of the post-Sullan prytany inscriptions honouring the Treasurer of the prytaneis.
[11] Vv. 60-74.
[12] *H.* xl 101-2, 3, *s.* i (?84/3), is restored in the same way.

name of the archon is extended in this period. Since there appears to be no particular reason for so doing, this practice may simply reflect Roman influence on Greek nomenclature:

(i) archon with patronymic: ii²1046 (Sokolowski [1969] 44), 52/1:

ἐπὶ Λυ|σάνδρου τοῦ [13] Ἀπολήξιδος ἄρχοντος

(ii) archon with demotic: *S.* xxi 499, A.D. 27/8:

[ἐπὶ Θεμιστο]κλέους Μαραθωνίου [ἄρχοντος

cf. the more elaborate ii²1072, bet. A.D. 91/2 and 97/8:

Ἐπὶ Τίτου Κωπωνίου, ἱεροκήρυκος υἱοῦ,[14] Μαξίμου Ἁγνουσίου ἄρχοντος

In all three of these examples note that the qualifying words intervene *between* the archon's name and the word ἄρχοντος. In contrast ii²1077 (Ag.xv 460), A.D. 209/10, is restored in an order:

[Ἐπὶ ἄρχοντος] Φλ. Διογένους Μαραθωνίου

which is reminiscent of the instances of ἄρχων - -, which we discussed above.[15] Cf. also *S.* xvi 103, A.D. 115/116: [Ἐπὶ ἄρχοντος Φλαο]υίου Μακρί|[νου Ἀχαρνέω]ς.

(iii) archon with phrase τοῦ μετὰ - -: [16] ii²1047, 49/8:

[Ἐπὶ Δημοχάρους ἄρχοντος τοῦ με]τὰ Δημήτριον

possibly to distinguish Demochares from the homonym of 108/7, though the interval in time seems rather great.

(3) Secretary: The secretary is omitted from two prescripts.[17] More significantly, we now find a variation in the time-honoured formula ἧι - - - - - ἐγραμμάτευεν: in ii²1077 (Ag.xv 460), A.D. 209/10, the latest example of the formulation,[18] we read:

[13] The article is, of course, *de rigueur* when the nomen is also in the genitive.

[14] ἱεροκήρυκος υἱός is added to distinguish the archon from his father, who is mentioned later as the proposer of the decree. For T. Coponius Maximus the 'sacred herald' and his son the archon, see J. H. Oliver, *GRBS* xiv 1973, 395-399. For the date of the son's archonship, see Simone Follet, *Mélanges . . . P. Chantraine*, Paris, 1972, 41-44.

[15] See p. 55.

[16] Cf. pp. 82-83 above.

[17] ii²1039 (*S.* xxii 110), 79/8; ii²1043, ?37/6 (privately published); cf. also *ASAA*² iii-v 83-7, 6, 75/4.

[18] ii²1078 (Sokolowski [1969] 8), A.D. 221/2, is in 'old style.'

ἧς ἐγραμμάτευεν Ῥόδων Καλλίστου Μαρα|[θώνιος,

the relative pronoun appearing in the genitive and the verb preceding the name of the official.[19] Cf. also *S.* xvi 103, A.D. 115/116 and *S.* xxi 504, *paullo post* A.D. 196, both of which show the same form and arrangement.

(4) Dating: The prytany date is omitted once.[20]

(5) Enacting body and place of meeting: There are two examples of formulae recording the transferring of a meeting from A to B. The clearest of these is ii^{2}1043, ?37/6:

β]ουλὴ ἐν τῶι θεάτρῳ ἡ [μεταχ]θεῖσα ἐκ τοῦ Πα[ναθ]
[η]ναϊκοῦ σταδίου·

In ii^{2}1039 (*S.* xxii 110), 79/8, we find a greatly abbreviated formula for a meeting of the boule transferred from the (Panathenaic) Stadium to the Theseion:

ἐ]ν τῶι Θησε[ίωι ἐκ] σταδ[ίου] [21]

(6) Chairman: This item is omitted in ii^{2}1039 (*S.* xxii 110), 79/8.[22]

Of much greater interest are two inscriptions where the chairman appears without his patronymic: [23]

ii^{2}1043, ?37/6:

τ[ῶν προέδρ]ων ἐπεψήφιζεν Δίω[ν . . .^{6}. . . ε]ὺς [κ]αὶ συμπρόεδροι·

ii^{2}1072, bet. A.D. 91/2 and 97/8:

τῶν προέδρων ἐπεψήφιζεν Ἡράκλειτος Πειριεὺς καὶ συνπρόεδροι·

Note also ii^{2}1077 (Ag.xv 460), A.D. 209/10, where the chairman loses his demotic and the article is attached to συμπρόεδροι:

---

[19] Presumably with the sense "of which the secretary was · · ·."

[20] In the otherwise unusual ii^{2}1039 (S. xxii 110), 79/8. Cf. also a transcript of an Athenian decree found in Lemnos: *ASAA*^{2} iii-v 83-7, 6, 75/4, in which the month appears in the genitive without specification of the day and the prytany date is entirely omitted.

[21] In *H.* xl 101-2, 3, *s.* i (?84/3), only the phrase ἡ μεταχθεῖσα can actually be read.

[22] Cf. also *ASAA*^{2} iii-v 83-7, 6, 75/4.

[23] Cf. also a transcript from Epidauros, *I.G.* iv^{2}, 1, 84, *c.* A.D. 40-42: τῶν προέδρων ἐπιψήφιζε (sic) Πλάτων Ἡφιστιάδης (sic) καὶ συνπρόεδροι.

τῶν προέδρων ἐπεψή|[φιζεν] Ἰουλιανὸς Κασίου καὶ οἱ συμπρόεδροι.[24]

(7) Enactment formula and minute-headings: The enactment formula is omitted in 4 instances.[25] In one of these [26] the minute-heading βουλῆς ψηφίσματα occurs.

(8) Orator: Normally this item appears in its usual form, NPD εἶπεν. Two instances, however, require comment:

ii²1072, bet. A.D. 91/2 and 97/8, where the orator is given a not inconsiderable prominence:

ὁ ἐπὶ τὰ ὅπλα στρα
τηγὸς τὸ δεύτερον καὶ γυμνασίαρχος τὸ δεύτερον καὶ ἱερεὺς Ἄρεως Ἐνυαλίου καὶ Ἐνυοῦς
καὶ Διὸς Γελέοντος ἱεροκῆρυξ Τίτος Κωπώνιος Μάξιμος Ἁγνούσιος εἶπεν·[27]

and ii²1078 (Sokolowski [1969] 8), A.D. 221/2, where the orator is stripped of his patronymic and demotic [28] but given a qualifying phrase:

Δ]ρυαντιανὸς ἄρχων [τῶν Εὐμολπιδῶν εἶπεν]·

In *S.* xxi 504 (honours for Julia Domna), *paullo post* A.D. 196, the orator is preceded by a qualifying phrase: vv. 4-5:

κατὰ τὴν ἐξήγησιν τοῦ πυ]θοχρήστου ἐξη[γητοῦ ------]
[---- Ἐλπιδηφόρος --- άδου Παλληνεὺ]ς εἶπεν.[29]

C. *Curtailed prescripts*

In the post-Sullan period we find a great many prytany inscriptions in which the prescript is entirely omitted.[30] The date is con-

[24] Cf. ii²545, ?321/0, pp. 39-41 above. The phenomenon is also restored in *S.* xxi 504, *paullo post* A.D. 196.

[25] ii²1039 (*S.* xxii 110), 79/8; ii²1043, ?37/6; ii²1072, between A.D. 91/2 and 97/8; ii²1077 (Ag.xv 460), A.D. 209/10. Cf. also *ASAA*² iii-v 83-7, 6, 75/4; *I.G.* iv², 1, 84, *c.* A.D. 40-42.

[26] ii²1039 (*S.* xxii 110), v. 2.

[27] For T. Coponius Maximus the 'sacred herald' see J. H. Oliver, *loc. cit.* (note 14 above).

[28] As properly in old style formulation.

[29] For the name of the orator and the restoration in v. 4 see *H.* xxxiii 1964, 200-1.

[30] ii²1050 (Ag.xv 264), *c.* 80/79; ii²1049 (Ag.xv 268), 57/6; Ag.xv 278, *m. s.* i; ii²1048 (Ag.xv 281), 46/5; Ag.xv 289, *c.* 30-20; Ag.xv 291, 21/0; Ag.xv 295, *aet.Aug.*; Ag.xv 301, *fin.s.* i; ii²1070 (Ag.xv 304), *paullo ante* A.D. 19; Ag.xv 306, *s.* i *a/p*; Ag.xv 316, *s.* i/ii*p.*

veyed solely by the mention of the year (by archon) in which the prytaneis were serving. These are all decrees of the boule, awarding honours to the Treasurer of the prytaneis. Dow [31] claims, justly, that these documents "bespeak a new age." Evidently at this period it was felt quite unnecessary to take the time and trouble (?expense) to inscribe full prescripts on monuments of this nature.[32]

There are, however, exceptions to this epigraphic austerity:

(1) Ag.xv 266, 64/3, atypically offers a full prescript, including the new heading:

[ἀγ]αθῆι τύχηι τῆς β[ου]λῆς καὶ [τοῦ δήμου τοῦ 'Αθηναίων].

(2) Ag.xv 292 Face A, 21/20, prefaces the text with mention of the στρατηγὸς ἐπὶ τὰ ὅπλα:

['Αγαθῆ τύχῃ· ἐπὶ τὰ ὅπλα στρατηγο]ῦντος 'Αντι⟦Σ̣⟧
[πάτρου τοῦ ͻ Φλυέως τὸ ⊥ ⟦] ` Λ̣ Σ̣Υ⟧

(3) Ag.xv 293, *c.* 20, and ii²1073 + 1074 (Ag.xv 322), *c.* A.D. 120, preface the text with the mover of the decree: [33]

Ag.xv 293: 'Απόληξις Φιλοκράτους ἐξ Οἴου εἶπεν·
Ag.xv 322: Φειδίας ͻ ['Ραμνούσιος γραμματεὺς τῶν πρυτάνεων? εἶπεν].

D. *Unusual prescripts*

(1) ii²1069 + 1119 (*S.* xxiv 143), *aet.imp.Aug.*: Honorary decree for Julius Nikanor. Unfortunately this text is extremely fragmentary but it reveals several unusual features:

'Αγαθῆι τύχηι τοῦ Σεβαστοῦ Καίσαρος Κ̣[------------- ἐπὶ]
Λάκωνος ἄρχοντος καὶ ἱερέως Δρούσο[υ ὑπάτου ---------------·]
ἐκκλησία ἐπὶ τῆς ἐννάτης (sic) πρυτανεί[ας ----------· τῶν προ]
έδρων ἐπεψήφιζεν Εὐθύδομος 'Α[-------------------------]

---

[31] *Prytaneis* p. 25.

[32] Cf. the ephebic texts of the same period where the second and third decrees of Reinmuth's 'Series B' texts (see *H.* xxxiv 1965, 264-7) may also be totally without prescript: ii²1039 (*S.* xxii 110), 79/8; ii²1041, 45/4; ii²1043 III, ?37/6.

[33] Dow's "modified post-Sullan 'second' decree": see *Prytaneis*, p. 197. Cf. also the ephebic texts, ii²1042, 40/39 (all three decrees introduced by the orator alone), and ii²1043 II and IV, ?37/6 (the fourth text of this document is one in honour of Sosis, who put up the entire monument as a dedication at his own expense).

(i) v. 1 is clearly an expression of general good fortune for the emperor.

(ii) for the functioning of the archon as the priest of Drusus cf. *I.G.* iv^2, 1, 84, *c.* A.D. 40-42:

ἐπὶ Σεκούνδου ἄρχοντος καὶ ἱερέως Δρούσου ὑπάτου

and the note there: "Archontes Attici simul Drusi sacerdotio functi sunt inde ab a. Chr. 9 usque ad Hadriani aetatem."

(iii) note how the meeting formula has been combined with the reference to the prytany.

(iv) vv. 4-5 continue with a reference to the Areopagos and the Council of the 600, but this should not be taken to imply a new procedure of joint meetings of the three corporations. It seems from the position in which the references occur that the Areopagos and the Council of the 600 are being mentioned among the considerations, possibly being cited as precedents. This text is a decree of the ecclesia alone.[34]

(2) ii^{2}1072, bet. A.D. 91/2 and 97/8: we have already cited this text with reference to the archon and orator items. It is also worthy of note in respect of the unusual sequence of the items of the prescript: archon—month date—prytanising tribe—prytany date—secretary—meeting heading—chairman—orator:

'Επὶ Τίτου Κωπωνίου, ἱεροκήρυκος υἱοῦ, Μαξίμου 'Αγνουσίου ἄρχοντος, Βοηδρ[ομιῶνος]
ὀγδόῃ μετ' εἰκάδα, ἐπὶ τῆς 'Αντιοχίδος τρίτης πρυτανείας, πεντεκαιδεκάτῃ τῆς
πρυτανείας, ᾗ Νεικίας Δωρίωνος Φλυεὺς ἐγραμμάτευεν· βουλὴ ἱερὰ ἐν 'Ελευσεινί[ωι]·
τῶν προέδρων ἐπεψήφιζεν 'Ηράκλειτος Πειριεὺς καὶ συνπρόεδροι· ὁ ἐπὶ τὰ ὅπλα στρα
τηγὸς τὸ δεύτερον καὶ γυμνασίαρχος τὸ δεύτερον καὶ ἱερεὺς ῎Αρεως 'Ενυαλίου καὶ 'Ενυοῦς
καὶ Διὸς Γελέοντος ἱεροκῆρυξ Τίτος Κωπώνιος Μάξιμος 'Αγνούσιος εἶπεν·

(3) ii^{2}1077 (Ag.xv 460), A.D. 209/10: a decree in honour of the

[34] Even if subject to the approval of the other two bodies: see Daniel J. Geagan, *The Athenian Constitution after Sulla, H.* Suppl. xii 1967, Chap. V *passim.*

imperial house of Septimius Severus, passed in a meeting of the boule convoked ἐπὶ τοῖς [εὐαγγ]ελίοις,[35] and based on a γνώμη (or 'proposal') of all three corporations viz. "the boule of the Areopagos, the boule of the 500 and the demos of the Athenians." [36] The prescript—perhaps not unexpectedly—is somewhat idiosyncratic: [37]

['Επὶ ἄρχοντος] Φλ. Διογένους Μαραθωνίου ἐπὶ τῆς Πανδιονί
[δος δ̄ πρυ]τανείας ἧς ἐγραμμάτευεν 'Ρόδων Καλλίστου Μαρα
[θώνιος]· ἱερε[ὺ]ς Θεόφιλος ἐπεστάτει· τῶν προέδρων ἐπεψή
[φιζεν] 'Ιουλιανὸς Κασίου καὶ οἱ συμπρόεδροι· ϰ̣γ τῆς πρυτα
[νείας], μηνὸς Ποσειδεῶνος τῇ ει̅· βουλὴ συνήχθη ἐπὶ τοῖς
[εὐαγγ]ελίοις, ἀναδειχθέντος ⟦Αὐτοκράτορος Καίσαρος Ποπλίου⟧
⟦Σεπτιμίου Γέτα Εὐσεβοῦς Σεβαστοῦ⟧· ἐν ᾗ ἀνεγνώσθη
[γνώμ]η [τ]ῶν συνεδρίων διὰ τῶν ἀρχόν[τ]ων, ἀναγνόν
[τος τοῦ] στρατηγοῦ 'Αλκαμένους Λαμπτρέως γνώμην τὴν ἀναγεγραμμένη[ν]·
['Η ἐξ 'Αρείου] πάγου βουλὴ καὶ ἡ βουλὴ τῶν Φ καὶ ὁ δῆμος ὁ 'Αθηναί
[ων μετὰ] τῶν ἀρχόντων, τοῦ τε ἐπωνύμου ἄρχοντος Φλ. Διογένους
[Μαραθων]ίου κα[ὶ τ]οῦ ἐπὶ τὰ ὅπλα στρατηγοῦ καὶ ἐπιμελητοῦ γυ
[μνασιαρχί]ας θε[οῦ] 'Αδρι[α]νοῦ καὶ ἀ[ντ]άρχοντος τοῦ ἱερωτάτου 'Ατ
[τικοῦ Π]ανε̣λ̣ληνίου [Μά]ρ. Αὐρ. 'Αλκαμένους Λαμπτρέως καὶ τοῦ κήρ
[υκος τῆς ἐξ] 'Αρε̣ίου π[ά]γου βουλῆς καὶ ἀγωνοθέτου τῶν τῆς Σεβα
[στῆς οἰκίας? ἀ]γώνω[ν Τρύ]φωνος τοῦ Θεοφίλου 'Υβάδου γνώμην ἀπο
[φαίνου]σιν κατὰ [τὰ] πάτρια· *vacat* 'Επειδὴ κτλ.

Clearly the circumstances of this decree contribute towards the

[35] The "good tidings" were news of the association of Geta in the empire with his father Septimius Severus and his brother Caracalla.

[36] See Geagan, *op. cit.*, 161-2, who argues that the participation of the other corporations is to be explained with reference to their cooperation in framing the γνώμη. Special procedures seem to have been in force governing decrees of honours for the imperial house, and this may help to explain the boule's passing of a decree based on the γνώμη of the synedria.

[37] I quote the text of Ag.xv 460. For the new restorations in vv. 2 and 5 see now Meritt, *H.* xliii 1974, 460-6. For a translation see J. H. Oliver, *Marcus Aurelius: Aspects of Civic and Cultural Policy in the East*, *H.* Suppl. xiii 1970, 111-112.

unusual form of the prescript. In vv. 7-10, where we might have expected to find the orator, it is recorded that a γνώμη of the synedria was read to this meeting of the boule. Vv. 10-17, in themselves tantamount to a formula naming the proposer of a motion, introduce this γνώμη, which is finally expressed in the remaining lines of the inscription.

Note also the following points:

(i) the ἱερεύς, who is the epistates (v. 3), presumably took the chair at this meeting. He takes precedence (in the list) over the epistates of the proedroi, but he does not put the motion to the vote.[38]

(ii) the date by prytany and by month [39] is postponed till after the chairman item. The new restorations give an equation

Posideon 15 = Prytany [IV] 23 = 104th day of the year

indicating that the Hadrianic year, which began in Boedromion, was still in use in the early third century.[40]

---

[38] Cf. *S.* xxi 504, *paullo post* A.D. 196, where v. 2 has been similarly restored: [ἱερεὺς ------ ἐπεστάτει].

[39] I.e. the reverse order of the norm. (For μηνὸς Ποσειδεῶνος cf. above pp. 91-92).

[40] In use, that is, at least for the Council of the 500.

CHAPTER EIGHT

EPILOGUE

From a descriptive study of this kind it is virtually impossible to draw anything which might reasonably be called a conclusion. However, there are, perhaps, certain salient features amid all the mass of documentation of the previous pages worthy of final consideration.

In the first place it should by now have become apparent that the Athenian prescript never actually achieved a fixed and final pattern. Certainly it gradually developed a very stereotyped form which, from the end of the fourth century, was more or less adhered to by the recording secretaries. But even to the very last years of our extant evidence variation and experimentation continued.

This is not to suggest that there was never anything approaching a paradigm: that there undoubtedly was, embracing the canonical items which the chancery style had embodied in the fifth and fourth centuries. Nevertheless it is true to state that, at any given period the secretary *qua* drafter was never *bound* to include all the items then at this disposal. He could—and did—make his own choice, whether to employ the 'full' stock prescript, or to reduce it by omitting one or more items: and, as far as we can tell, this was his privilege.

This leads us to a second point viz. that the Athenian secretaries clearly had much greater discretion in deciding how to frame the minutes of the meetings they attended than do their modern counterparts. No rigid standards or narrow guidelines of secretarial practice seem to have been imposed, so that, to some extent, the secretary was a free agent in deciding how to lay out his text in preparation for publication on stone. And, as we have seen, this freedom extended not only to a choice among the canonical items but to a decision—admittedly within narrower limits—on the order and form in which the items were to be expressed.

Secretaries were also not infrequently guilty of carelessness, for example in describing the nature of the meeting or of the enacting body, a carelessness which would hardly be tolerated in the publication of modern acts of parliament. Moreover, their collaborators in publication, the masons, were also not above making a few blunders in the finished article on stone, blunders which they may have deliberately left uncorrected for purely aesthetic reasons. But neither party should be too severely censured: we must not apply modern standards to ancient practice, nor must we forget that the recorders of the ancient world had to make do with a somewhat more primitive technology than that available today.

And not only that. This lack of precision which so offends our senses may in fact have been quite acceptable in the Athenian state. This supposition is perhaps borne out by examples of quotation in literary sources of documents which we also possess on stone: it is quite clear that *verbatim* accuracy was neither demanded nor expected. The ancient attitude to the recording of documents, whether on stone or some less durable material, was very different from ours: provided the essential information was conveyed, complete fidelity of reproduction just did not enter into it. This is surely totally predictable in a society which did not possess the printing press: every copy of any text was to some degree unique.

One final comment. Down to the end of the fourth century the development of the prescript proceeded along orderly and logical lines: from the simple statement of legal sanction, through a period when the function of the prescript was simply to record the responsible officials, to a time when the greater publicity given to stones no longer confined to the Acropolis occasioned the refinement of details of date and venue. From the third century, however, such refinements became more trivial and contributed little or nothing to the essential information of the prescript. This was a display of interest in form for the sake of form, not a deepfelt need for improvement on the existing pattern, and doubtless reflects the growing concern with the outward show of government as opposed to the practice of real power, an outward show best seen in the increasingly fulsome tributes of the countless honorary decrees to which these prescripts are so often attached.

As in many countries of western Europe today, so likewise in the period of Athens' declining fortunes, the less vigorous the society, the more pretentious and complex the administrative machine.

APPENDIX I

THE ARCHON LISTS

The dating of a text naming an archon is, of course, dependent on our being able to assign that archon to his precise year of office. The archon lists are now established on a fundamentally sound basis well into the Hellenistic period.

The lists can be most conveniently consulted in the following sources:

(1) 500-403: ML p. 291
(2) 403-323: Tod, vol. ii, p. 316
(3) 347/6-48/7: see B.D. Meritt, "Athenian Archons 347/6-48/7", *Historia* (forthcoming).
(4) 46/5-: the following selective list is compiled from a variety of sources. The principle of selection is whether or not a given archon appears in a prescript of a decree of the boule or ecclesia.

Year	*Archon*	*Reference*
46/5	Apolexis	*BCH* xc 1966, 93-100
?37/6	Kallikratides	Dinsmoor *AA*, pp. 280-6
21/0	Apolexis	*BCH* xc 1966, 93-100
A.D.		
27/8	Themistokles	ii²1713
c. 40-42	Secundus	iv², 1, 84
between 91/2 and 97/8	T. Coponius Maximus of Hagnous	Follet, *Mélanges . . . P. Chantraine*, p. 43
115/116	Flavius Makreinos of Acharnai	*eadem, loc. cit.*
209/10	Flavius Diogenes	*H.* xviii 1949, 3 and 19
221/2	Arabianos	*H.* xviii 1949, 37-9

APPENDIX II

SOME FIRST OCCURRENCES

Item	*Reference*	*Date*
archon in prescript	$i^2$19 + 20 vv. 1-2 (BM pp. 71-2)	458/7
secretary with demotic in superscript	*S.* x 15	*c.* 450
secretary with patronymic in superscript	$i^2$57 (ML 65)	424/3
secretary with demotic in prescript	?$i^2$72 (*S.* x 88)	*c.* 423/2 [1]
secretary with both patronymic and demotic in superscript	$i^2$82	421/0
archon in superscript (ἐπὶ τοῦ δεῖνος ἄρχοντος)	$i^2$84 (Sokolowski [1969] 13)	421/0
archon in superscript (ὁ δεῖνα ἦρχε)	$i^2$115 (ML 86)	409/8
archon with demotic in superscript (ὁ δεῖνα demotic ἦρχεν)	$i^2$124	406/5
epistates with demotic (ὁ δεῖνα ἐπεστάτε)	$i^2$125	405/4
archon in prescript (ἐπὶ τοῦ δεῖνος ἄρχοντος)	$ii^2$18 (Tod 108)	394/3
prytanising tribe with ordinal	*ibidem*	394/3
secretary with patronymic and demotic in prescript—old style	$ii^2$16 (Tod 103)	394/3
secretary with patronymic and demotic in prescript—new style	$ii^2$18 (Tod 108)	394/3
τῶν προέδρων ἐπεψήφιζεν ὁ δεῖνα + demotic	$ii^2$44 (Tod 124)	378/7
number of day of prytany	$ii^2$105 + 523 (Tod 136)	368/7
orator with patronymic and demotic	$ii^2$136	354/3
number of day of month	$ii^2$229 (*c.* Add. p. 659)	341/0
type of meeting	$ii^2$330 III	336/5
mention of καὶ συμπρόεδροι (+ names)	$ii^2$336 III (*c.* Add. p. 659)	333/2
anagrapheus	*S.* xxi 303	321/0
τῶν προέδρων ἐπεψήφιζεν ὁ δεῖνα with patronymic and demotic	$ii^2$450	314/13
archon with demotic	$ii^2$665	266/5

[1] First surely attested instance $i^2$47 (*S.* x 136), 407/6: but see above p. 6.

'perfect design'	ii²778	250/49
minute-headings	ii²832	229/8
'triple dating'	*S.* xxv 112	196/5
archon ὁ μετὰ -	ii²916 I and II	192/1
antigrapheus	ii²967 (Ag.xv 238)	145/4
ἀγαθῆι τύχηι in superscript	ii²1009	116/5
ἀγαθῆι τύχηι in prescript	ii²1011 I	106/5
strategos epi ta hopla	ii²1039 (*S.* xxii 110)	79/8
ἀγαθῆι τύχηι τῆς βουλῆς καὶ τοῦ δήμου τοῦ Ἀθηναίων	Ag.xv 266	64/3
archon with patronymic	ii²1046 (Sokolowski [1969] 44)	52/1

BIBLIOGRAPHY

Mere publications or re-publications of epigraphical texts are, for the most part, excluded from this list.

Austin, R. P., *The Stoichedon Style in Greek Inscriptions*, O.U.P., 1938.

Berve, H., *Die Tyrannis bei den Griechen*, 2 vols., Munich: Beck, 1967.

Bingen, J., "Préambule et Promoteur dans le Décret Attique," *Le Monde Grec: pensée, littérature, histoire, documents: Hommages à Claire Préaux*, Univ. of Brussels, 1975, 470-9.

Bradeen, D. W. and McGregor, M. F., *Studies in Fifth-Century Attic Epigraphy*, University of Oklahoma Press, 1973.

Brillant, M., *Les secrétaires athéniens*, (Bibl. de l'École des Hautes Études, 191), Paris: Champion, 1911.

Busolt, G., revised by Swoboda, H., *Griechische Staatskunde*, 2 vols. (*Handbuch der Altertumswissenschaft*, iv.1.1), Munich: Beck, 1920/6.

Cadoux, T. J., "The Athenian Archons from Kreon to Hypsichides," *JHS* lxviii 1948, 70-123.

De Laix, R. A., *Probouleusis at Athens: A Study of Political Decision-Making*, (Univ. of California Publications in History, vol. 83), Univ. of California Press, 1973.

Dinsmoor, W. B., *The Archons of Athens in the Hellenistic Age*, Harvard U.P. for A.S.C.S.A., 1931.

——, *The Athenian Archon List in the Light of Recent Discoveries*, Columbia U.P., 1939.

Dow, S., "New Kinds of Evidence for Dating Polyeuktos," *AJA* xl 1936, 57-70.

——, *Prytaneis*, *Hesperia* Suppl. i 1937.

——, "Archons of the Period after Sulla," *Hesperia* Suppl. viii 1949, 116-125.

——, "The Athenian Anagrapheis," *HSCP* lxvii 1963, 37-54.

——, "Three Athenian Decrees: Method in the Restoration of Preambles," *HSCP* lxvii 1963, 55-75.

——, "The Preambles of Athenian Decrees containing Lists of Symproedroi," *Hesperia* xxxii 1963, 335-65.

Druet, F.-X., "Le Préambule des Décrets Attiques," *Rev. Belge de Phil. et d'Hist.* xlix 1971, 73-83.

Ferguson, W. S., *The Athenian Secretaries*, (Cornell Studies in Classical Philology, vii), New York: Macmillan for Cornell Univ., 1898.

——, *Hellenistic Athens*, Macmillan, 1911.

——, "The Introduction of the Secretary Cycle," *Klio* xiv 1914-15, 393-7.

——, *Athenian Tribal Cycles*, (Harvard Historical Monographs, i), Harvard U.P., 1932.

Follet, S., "Flavius Euphanès d'Athènes, ami de Plutarque," *Mélanges de Linguistique et de Philologie Grecques offerts à Pierre Chantraine*, (Études et Commentaires, lxxix), Paris, 1972, 35-50.

Geagan, D. J., *The Athenian Constitution after Sulla, Hesperia* Suppl. xii 1967.
Glotz, G., "L'épistate des proèdres," *REG* xxxiv 1921, 1-19.
Graindor, P., *Chronologie des archontes athéniens sous l'Empire*, Mem. Acad. Belg., 2nd. ser., viii 2 1922.
——, *Athènes sous Auguste*, (Rec. Fac. Lett., i), Cairo: Misr for Univ. of Egypt, 1927.
——, *Athènes de Tibère à Trajan*, (Rec. Fac. Lett., viii), Cairo: Misr for Univ. of Egypt, 1931.
——, *Athènes sous Hadrien*, Cairo: Ministry of Public Instruction, 1934.

Hartel, W., "Studien über attisches Staatsrecht und Urkundenwesen," *Sb. Wien* xc.3, May 1878, 543-624; xci.1, June 1878, 101-94; xcii.1, October 1878, 87-184; also published separately, Vienna: Gerold, 1878.
Hill, G. F., revised by Meiggs, R. and Andrewes, A., *Sources for Greek History between the Persian and Peloponnesian Wars*, O.U.P., 1951.
Hondius, J. J. E., *Novae Inscriptiones Atticae*, Leiden: Sijthoff, 1925.

Kirchner, J., *Prosopographia Attica*, 2 vols., Berlin: Reimer, 1901/3.
Klaffenbach, G., *Griechische Epigraphik*,[2] (Studienhefte zur Altertumswissenschaft, vi), Göttingen: Vandenhoeck & Ruprecht, 1966.

Lambrechts, A., *Texts en Uitzicht van de Atheense Proxeniedecreten tot 323 v.C.*, (K.V.Ac. Wetenschappen, Klasse der Letteren, xxxii), Brussels: Paleis der Academiën, 1958. (In Flemish: summary in French.)
Laqueuer, R., *Epigraphische Untersuchungen zu den griechischen Volksbeschlüssen*, Leipzig and Berlin: Teubner, 1927.
Larfeld, W., *Handbuch der griechischen Epigraphik*, vol. II ii, Leipzig: Reisland, 1902.
——, *Griechische Epigraphik*,[3] (*Handbuch der Altertumswissenschaft*, i.5), Munich: Beck, 1914.
Lewis, D. M., "Notes on Attic Inscriptions, vi. The Epistates of the Proedroi," *BSA* xlix 1954, 31-4.
Luria, S., "Zur Geschichte der Präskripten in den attischen voreuklidischen Volksbeschlüssen," *Hermes* lxii 1927, 257-75.

McDonald, W. A., *The Political Meeting Places of the Greeks*, (Johns Hopkins Studies in Archaeology, xxxiv), Baltimore: Johns Hopkins Press, 1943.
McGregor, M. F., "Method and Manners in Greek Epigraphy," *Phoenix* xx 1966, 210-27.
Mattingly, H. B., "Athens and Eleusis: Some New Ideas," *Φόρος: Tribute to Benjamin Dean Meritt*, Locust Valley, New York, Augustin, 1974.
Meiggs, R. and Lewis, D. M., *A Selection of Greek Historical Inscriptions to the End of the Fifth Century B.C.*, O.U.P., 1969.
Meisterhans, K., revised by Schwyzer, E., *Grammatik der attischen Inschriften*,[3] Berlin: Weidmannsche Buchhandlung, 1900.
Meritt, B. D., *Athenian Financial Documents of the Fifth Century*, (Humanistic Series, xxvii), Univ. of Michigan Press, 1932.
——, "The Archonship of Symmachos," *AJP* lxxviii 1957, 375-81.
——, *The Athenian Year*, (Sather Lectures, xxxii), Univ. of California Press, 1961.
——, "The Year of Neaichmos (320/19 B.C.)," *Hesperia* xxxii 1963, 425-38.
——, "Chronology of the Late Fourth Century," *Hesperia* xxxiii 1964, 1-15.
——, "Athenian Calendar Problems," *TAPA* xcv 1964, 200-60.

——, "Polyeuktos and Philoneos," *The Classical Tradition: Literary and Historical Studies in Honor of H. Caplan*, Cornell U.P., 1966, 26-42.
——, "Calendar Studies," 'Αρχ. 'Εφ. cvii 1968 (publ. 1969), 77-115.
——, "Metonic Intercalations in Athens," *Hesperia* xxxviii 1969, 107-13.
——, "The Election of Athenian Generals," *Klio* lii 1970, 277-82.
——, "The Chronology of the Peloponnesian War," *Proc. Amer. Philos. Soc.* cxv 1971, 97-124.
——, "Two Attic Decrees of the Late Fourth Century," *AJP* xciii 1972, 164-8.
——, "The Athenian Calendar Again," 'Αρχ. 'Εφ. cxii 1973, 237-45.
——, "The Year of Archippos at Athens (318/7 B.C.)," *Hesperia* xlv 1976, 173.
——, "Athenian Archons 347/6-48/7," *Historia* (forthcoming).
—— and Traill, J. S., *The Athenian Agora, xv: Inscriptions: The Athenian Councillors*, A.S.C.S.A., Princeton, 1974.
—— and Wade-Gery, H. T., "The Dating of Documents to the Mid-Fifth Century," *JHS* lxxxii 1962, 67-74: *ibid.* lxxxiii 1963, 100-17.
——, Wade-Gery, H. T. and McGregor, M. F., *The Athenian Tribute Lists*, 4 vols., Harvard U.P. for A.S.C.S.A. (vol. i); Princeton: A.S.C.S.A. (vols. ii-iv), 1939/49/50/53.
Miller, H. A. E. O., *De Decretis Atticis Quaestiones Epigraphicae*, Breslau: Grass, Barth, 1885.

Notopoulos, J. A., "Studies in the Chronology of Athens under the Empire," *Hesperia* xviii 1949, 1-57.

Oliver, J. H., "Greek Inscriptions: Appendix II: Athenian Archons under the Roman Empire," *Hesperia* xi 1942, 81-9.
——, *Marcus Aurelius: Aspects of Civil and Cultural Policy in the East*, *Hesperia* Suppl. xiii 1970.
Osborne, M. J., "Honours for Sthorys (*IG* ii², 17)," *BSA* lxv 1970, 151-74.
——, "Attic Citizenship Decrees: A Note," *BSA* lxvi 1971, 129-58.
——, "The Stoichedon Style in Theory and Practice," *ZPE* x 1973, 249-70.

Pečírka, J., *The Formula for the Grant of Enktesis in Attic Inscriptions*, Prague: *Acta Universitatis Carolinae, Phil. et Hist. Mon.* xv 1966.
Pritchett, W. K., *Ancient Athenian Calendars on Stone*, (Univ. of California Publications in Class. Arch., iv 4), Univ. of California Press, 1963.
——, "The Name of the Game is Restoration," *California Studies in Classical Antiquity* iii 1970, 199-214.
—— and Meritt, B. D., *The Chronology of Hellenistic Athens*, Harvard U.P. for A.S.C.S.A., 1940.
—— and Neugebauer, O., *The Calendars of Athens*, Harvard U.P. for A.S.C.S.A., 1947.

Reinmuth, O. W., "The Attic Archons Named Apolexis," *BCH* xc 1966, 93-100.
——, *The Ephebic Inscriptions of the Fourth Century B.C.*, *Mnemosyne* Suppl. xiv 1971.
——, "A New Ephebic Inscription from the Athenian Agora," *Hesperia* xliii 1974, 246-59.
Rhodes, P. J., *The Athenian Boule*, O.U.P., 1972.

Smith, S. B., "The Athenian Proedroi," *CP* xxv 1930, 250-76.
Sokolowski, F., *Lois sacrées des cités grecques* (*Supplément*), (École française d'Athènes: Travaux et Mémoires, xi), Paris: Boccard, 1962.
——, *Lois sacrées des cités grecques*, (École française d'Athènes: Travaux et Mémoires, xviii), Paris: Boccard, 1969.
Stroud, R. S., "An Athenian Law on Silver Coinage," *Hesperia* xliii 1974, 157-88.
Swoboda, H., *Die griechischen Volksbeschlüssen: epigraphische Untersuchungen*, Leipzig: Teubner, 1890.

Thiel, J. H., "De Voorzitter van de Atheense Volksvergadering," *Med. Nederl. Akad. van Wet.* xxviii 8, 1965, 433-41.
Tod, M. N., *A Selection of Greek Historical Inscriptions*, 2 vols., O.U.P., 1933 (2nd ed. 1946)/1948.
Traill, J. S., *The Political Organisation of Attica*, *Hesperia* Suppl. xiv 1975.
——, "A Revision of *Hesperia*, XLIII, 1974, 'A New Ephebic Inscription from the Athenian Agora'," *Hesperia* xlv 1976, 296-303.

Walbank, M. B., "New Readings in an Athenian Accounting Document: *I.G.*, I^2, 337," *Hesperia* xliv 1975, 435-41.
Woodhead, A. G., *The Study of Greek Inscriptions*, C.U.P., 1959.
——, *The Athenian Agora xvi: Inscriptions: Decrees and Ephebic Texts*, A.S.C.S.A., Princeton, (forthcoming).

INDEX OF EPIGRAPHICAL TEXTS CITED

GENERAL INDEX

www.ingramcontent.com/pod-product-compliance
Ingram Content Group UK Ltd.
Pitfield, Milton Keynes, MK11 3LW, UK
UKHW040650210926
15296UKWH00042B/684

9 789004 054295